JAMES E. ALLEN
100 E. Ocean View Ave. #808
Norfolk, VA 23503-1633

# SIGNING
## Naturally

# VISTA

## AMERICAN SIGN LANGUAGE SERIES
## FUNCTIONAL NOTIONAL APPROACH

# SIGNING
*Naturally*

## STUDENT
## WORKBOOK

### LEVEL

# 2

DawnSignPress
San Diego, California

Sign Illustrations by *Frank Allen Paul, Paul Setzer*
Illustrations by *Chuck Baird, Patricia Pearson, Valerie Winemiller*

SIGN MODELS

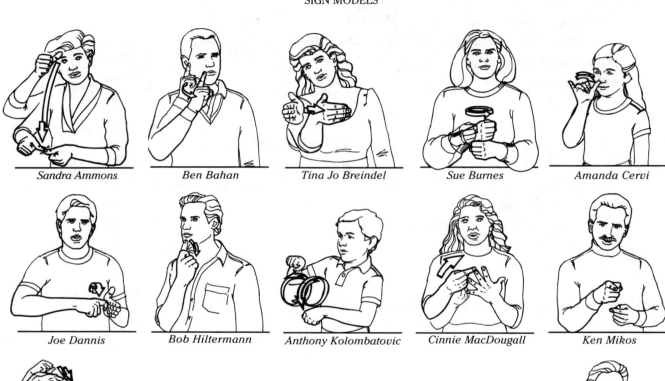

| | | | | |
|---|---|---|---|---|
| *Sandra Ammons* | *Ben Bahan* | *Tina Jo Breindel* | *Sue Burnes* | *Amanda Cervi* |
| *Joe Dannis* | *Bob Hiltermann* | *Anthony Kolombatovic* | *Cinnie MacDougall* | *Ken Mikos* |

*Erin Paul*

Published by DawnSignPress

ISBN: 0-915035-16-2

Printed in the United States of America

10  9  8  7  6  5  4  3  2

*Robin Taylor*

*Quantity discounts and special purchase arrangements
for teachers are available. For information, please contact:*

DᴀᴡɴSɪɢɴPʀᴇss
6130 Nancy Ridge Drive, San Diego, California  92121
(619) 626-0600 V/TTY   (619) 625-2336 FAX
ORDER TOLL FREE 1-800-549-5350

# TABLE OF CONTENTS

# INTRODUCTION

The *Signing Naturally: Student Videotext and Workbook, Level 2* are designed to provide you with an opportunity to review and practice what you learn in the classroom, as well as to increase your comprehension of signed narratives. A Vocabulary Review section is provided for reference at the end of each unit. There is no audio for the videotape.

The advantages of using a videotext along with a workbook and vocabulary are many:

- With videotape, you can see the movement of signs as they are used in a sentence.
- You can observe how a sign form is influenced by the sign that precedes or follows.
- You can learn how sign movements can be modified to change meaning.
- You can see when and how facial expressions occur.
- You can observe how body, head, and eye movements are used for phrasing and agreement.
- You can see how language is used in context.
- You can see how a visual language such as American Sign Language (ASL) can be used creatively in poetry, drama and storytelling.
- Best of all, you can rewind as many times as you wish to review what you have seen and to enjoy hours and hours of signed entertainment.

Each of the five units in Level 2 revolves around a major language function: locating things around the house; complaining and making requests; talking about life events, nationalities and family histories; describing objects; talking about the weekend. The language you learn through this communicative approach is the language used in everyday conversation. By learning language functions in interactive contexts, you also develop conversational skills in confirming and correcting information; opening and closing conversations; asking for clarification; agreeing, declining or hedging; and using appropriate response behaviors.

Specific language and cultural behaviors are introduced in the Cumulative Review unit at the end of Level 2. You will learn appropriate ways of getting and directing attention in various situations, controlling the pace of conversation, resuming the previous topic of conversation, and getting help with the spelling of names.

## Design of the *Videotext and Workbook*

The *Student Workbook* is designed to be a guide to the *Videotext*. Read the instructions in the workbook before beginning each videotaped activity. Then go back to the workbook for additional activities.

The units are divided into several sections:

**LANGUAGE IN ACTION**: Each unit begins with a videotaped conversation, which is accompanied in the workbook by a written dialogue that highlights specific language functions and key phrases taught in the unit. You may see signs or expressions in the videotaped conversation that are unfamiliar. We suggest you approach the conversation in the following stages:

1) Read the situation at the beginning of each dialogue in the workbook.
2) View the conversation and try to follow the intent of the exchange. Do not concern yourself with individual unfamiliar signs.
3) Read the dialogue in the workbook to see if you understood the exchange. Answer the questions or do the activity requested based on your understanding of the videotape.

4) View the conversation again, looking for how key phrases are expressed.

5) Rehearse the key phrases.

**LANGUAGE IN PRACTICE**: This is the largest section of each unit, and is structured as follows:

1) It begins with grammar notes that explain the grammar features introduced in the unit. Notes on narrative structure, sequencing principles, and transitions may also be included. These are followed by videotaped demonstrations of these grammar features.

2) Activities follow which give you an opportunity to identify and practice the grammar features introduced.

3) The bulk of the exercises that follow are comprehension activities that test your understanding of the vocabulary and language functions you have learned.

4) Then follow numbered demonstrations, numbered practice and fingerspelling comprehension practice.

5) Each Language in Practice section ends with The Story Corner, a videotaped story that is either humorous or informative. It is designed to help you build your receptive skills, learn vocabulary through context, and develop strategies for figuring out meaning without understanding every sign.

**LANGUAGE IN PERFORMANCE**: Each unit concludes with a Language in Performance section, in which you see creative and artistic uses of ASL. Noted ASL artists and actors perform in the following genres:

Unit 13: Handshape Stories

Unit 14: Cheers and Songs

Unit 15: Poetry

Unit 16: Storytelling

Unit 17: Legends

Cumulative Review: Units 13–17: Drama

Dr. Sam Supalla, a professor at the University of Arizona who is well known for his work as a filmmaker and ASL storyteller, will introduce each performer, giving background and cultural information on each piece presented. These ASL introductions use language appropriate for students at this level. We also include a written introduction to give you a more in-depth explanation of each piece.

**VOCABULARY REVIEW**: At the end of each unit in the workbook, you will find sign illustrations of key phrases and vocabulary for that unit. Many of the sign illustrations have a corresponding picture to show the meaning of the sign. Other more abstract vocabulary whose meaning cannot easily be illustrated with pictures are grouped into categories to help you remember the meaning of the sign. We chose not to give you English equivalents because they often restrict your understanding and usage of the signs.

Some signs vary from one region to the next. Your instructor may have introduced a different sign more commonly used in your local area than the one used in your workbook. Be sure to remember the local sign, but be aware that there will be different signs used in other parts of the United States and Canada.

**ANSWER KEY**: An Answer Key is provided at the back so that you can check your answers. Answers for all activities are given, as well as summaries of some of the videotaped narratives.

# How to Use the *Videotext and Workbook*

1) Since as much videotape time as possible has been used for language purposes, all instructions for videotaped activities are given in the workbook. Remember to read the instructions in the workbook before starting each activity.

2) Most activities on videotape allow a two- to three-second pause for you to mark your answers. This may not be enough time, so feel free to stop the tape to give yourself more time to answer. Avoid using the Pause button as this can cause damage to your tape.

3) If you miss a sign or sentence while working on an activity, don't rewind the tape to see just that part again, but continue the activity till the end, then replay the whole activity to complete the answers you missed. This way, you save time by not having to rewind repeatedly, and it saves wear and tear on the tape.

4) After you complete a workbook activity, check your answers in the Answer Key at the back of the book.

5) Also after each activity, you can replay the tape for additional language practice. For example, after identifying the verb forms used in videotaped sentences, go back and practice signing the sentences.

6) Use the *Videotext* as a reference to review and practice what you have learned, to prepare for tests, and to retain your Sign Language skills during breaks in school sessions.

# Signers on the *Videotext*

Nearly all of the signers on videotape are identified by their actual names in the workbook except when they are assuming another character. In order to follow the conversations in the Language in Action sections, it would be helpful for you to familiarize yourself with the names of the signers featured on the videotape:

Ethan Bernstein     Tina Jo Breindel     Ramona Galindez

Malcolm Grossinger

Ivanetta Ikeda

Marlon (Lon) Kuntze

Dan Lynch

Cinnie MacDougall

Joe MacDougall

Shane Marsh

Steve McCullough

Anthony Natale

Carlene Pedersen

Priscilla Poynor

Sandra Rasmus

Yolanda Roberson

Mary Hill Telford

Guy Wonder

Pat Zinkovich

## Language in Performance Signers

Ben Bahan

Ella Mae Lentz

Freda Norman

Sam Supalla

# SIGNING Naturally

# UNIT 13
# Locating Things Around the House

## LANGUAGE IN ACTION

## Describing the Layout of a Home

Read the situation below before watching the videotaped conversation "Describing the Layout of a Home." Then watch the tape and try to follow the intent of the exchange. You may see signs or expressions that are unfamiliar. Do not concern yourself with these, but let context and the conversation as a whole help you figure out the meaning. Refer to the dialogue below as necessary.

**Situation**: Yolanda, who plans to take a ski trip soon, is introduced to Guy to discuss the possibility of renting Guy's cabin in the mountains.

Yolanda:  
Priscilla: } greetings

Yolanda:  explains what she's been doing. Asks Priscilla if she knows of anyone with a cabin for rent

Priscilla:  responds affirmatively, tells Yolanda that the man sitting at the pool has a cabin, asks if she wants to check with him

Yolanda:  responds affirmatively

Priscilla:  (gets Guy's attention) explains that Yolanda is looking for a cabin to rent

Guy:  (to Yolanda) asks when she needs it

Yolanda:  tells when

Guy:  responds

Yolanda:  asks for information on the cabin

Guy:  **describes cabin**

Yolanda:  asks if the cabin has certain features

Guy:  responds

All:  closing

Watch Guy's use of space when he describes his cabin: observe how he uses different areas of his signing space to correspond to different areas of the cabin. Then fill in the information he gives about the cabin on the floor plan on the following page.

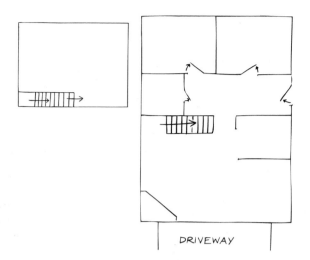

Answers on p. 155.

# LANGUAGE IN PRACTICE

## Telling Locations of Things in a Room

There are various ways to tell locations in ASL. In previous units you have practiced pointing to actual locations, i.e., down the hall to the right; practiced waving up, down, left or right; and learned certain expressions that relate one location to another, i.e., signs for next to, across from, near. You have learned to use non-manual behaviors (facial expressions) to add specific information about how close or how far away things are.

In this unit, we focus on describing the furniture arrangement in a room and on telling locations of objects.

## Using Classifiers to Tell Locations

One way to tell where things are located is by using certain signs called **classifiers**. Many languages use classifiers, usually to categorize nouns by certain shared characteristics. In ASL, classifiers are specific handshapes used to represent nouns according to their *shape*, i.e., flat objects, cylindrical objects; their *location*, i.e., on the wall, on a shelf; their *number* (often including how the things are arranged), i.e., many things stacked, several things in a row.*

The classifiers practiced in this unit are used to indicate the location of nouns such as furniture or other objects around the house. Each classifier is signed in the area of your signing space that corresponds to the object's location in the room. The classifier handshapes you use should agree with the general *shape* of the objects they represent, or with the *type* of object; they also may show how the object is *oriented* in the room.

Pictured on the following page are some of the classifier handshapes used for telling locations. Beneath each illustration we indicate in parentheses whether the classifier shows the shape, type, or orientation of the objects it represents. Then follow some examples of the nouns the classifier may represent. In the next videotaped segment, you will see these classifiers used to represent each noun listed.**

---

*ASL has other kinds of classifiers that are not introduced in this unit, including semantic, body, and bodypart classifiers, and classifiers that indicate how an object moves. The information about classifiers in this workbook is adapted from Ted Supalla's paper, "The Classifier System in American Sign Language," *Proceedings of the Fourth National Symposium on Sign Language Research and Teaching*, National Association of the Deaf, Silver Spring, Md., 1986.

**If you're not sure which classifier to use to represent an object, *point* to the corresponding location of your signing space instead. Pointing is always an acceptable way of referencing.

| (shape)<br>pictures on wall<br>cabinet doors | (shape and<br>orientation)<br>refrigerator<br>dishwasher<br>dresser | (shape and<br>orientation)<br>kitchen island<br>counter top<br>sink cabinet<br>sofa | (type and<br>orientation)<br>chair |
|---|---|---|---|
| (shape)<br>window<br>mirror | (shape and<br>orientation)<br>table<br>bed | (shape and<br>orientation)<br>long thin windows<br>built-in oven<br>grandfather clock | (type)<br>vase<br>potted plant<br>table lamp |

## Describing the Arrangement of a Room

ASL users often include information about spatial relationships when describing things. Describing physical arrangements requires skills in visualizing the room and in using the interplay of both hands to show where objects are located in relation to each other. Both these skills will help you convey an accurate image to your listener.

When you want to describe how a room looks, i.e., its shape, decor, or the arrangement of the furniture in it, follow this general sequence:

- Identify the room and begin your description from the perspective of the doorway.
- Describe the shape of the room, if it is unusual or relevant.
- Identify the furniture or features in the room, starting with the most noticeable, i.e., fireplace in a living room, island in a kitchen, bed in a bedroom.
- After identifying each feature or piece of furniture, indicate its location in the room or in relation to previously mentioned objects by using classifiers or pointing.
- Do the same for each part of the room using an orderly or logical sequence, i.e., from left to right, from near to far, or area by area.

## Room Description

Look at the four rooms illustrated below. Then, watch the descriptions of these rooms on videotape.* Notice the **sequence** of description. Write numbers on the appropriate furniture and features in each picture according to which items are mentioned first, second, third, etc.

Room Description 1: Number the items in the order described.

Room Description 2: Number the items in the order described.

*Rooms are not always described in the detail you will see on the videotape, depending on the purpose of the description. The examples on tape are presented for instructional purposes, so that you can master the grammar principles involved. You can see examples of how people describe rooms in everyday contexts in the dialogues in later segments of the videotape.

Room Description 3: Number the items in the order described.

Room Description 4: Number the items in the order described.

Answers on pp. 155–156.

**Indicating spatial relationships**. Notice how the signers use classifiers and pointing to establish locations. They use different areas of their signing space to correspond to different areas of the room, and describe certain objects in the correct spatial relationship to nearby objects. For example, in the description of the living room, Carlene indicates the spatial relationships among furniture within each area of the room. Some objects have a natural association, i.e., sofa with coffee table, desk with chair, chair with ottoman. After Carlene finishes her description, the listener should be able to visualize the arrangement of most, if not all, of the furniture in the room.

Also notice the signers' **eye gaze**: they look at you when they identify each object, and shift their gaze to the area where the object is located.

## Locating Small Objects

If you want to tell where an object is located, i.e., to have someone go get the object for you, the amount and kind of information you give is different from when you describe the arrangement of a room. To tell where an object is located, follow this general sequence:

- Identify what room the object is in. Visualize the room from the perspective of the doorway.
- Identify what part of the room the object is in, usually by indicating the nearest piece of furniture noticeable from the doorway.
- Continue to narrow down the location by using classifiers, signs or pointing, ending at the specific location of the object, i.e., next to the couch, in the end table, in the second drawer of the end table. Shift your eye gaze to each location as you identify it.
- Finally, indicate the object's exact location, usually by pointing.

### Minidialogues

In the next video segment, the same signers who described the room arrangements will tell the locations of certain objects in the same rooms. The locations they identify are marked with an "X" in the illustrations that follow.

Watch the four minidialogues. Notice how the details given to tell specific locations are different from those given to describe the arrangement of the rooms. The signers give just enough detail for the listener to understand exactly where the object is.

After watching each minidialogue, answer the questions below.

**Minidialogue 1**

1. What is Ethan looking for?

2. In what sequence does Mary tell the location? (For example: in the dining room, in the china cabinet, on the bottom shelf, on the left side.)

a)_____    c)_____

b)_____    d)_____

3. Judging by how they talk with each other, circle the kind of relationship they have:

      family      friends      strangers

### Minidialogue 2

**1.** What is Malcolm looking for?

**2.** In what sequence does Cinnie tell the location?

a)_____ c)_____

b)_____ d)_____

**3.** How does Malcolm confirm the location?

**4.** Circle the kind of relationship they have:

    family      friends      strangers

### Minidialogue 3

**1.** What is Dan looking for?

**2.** In what sequence does Priscilla tell the location?

    a) _____

    b) _____

    c) _____

**3.** Where did Dan think the location was at first?

**4.** Circle the kind of relationship they have:

    family      friends      strangers

### Minidialogue 4

**1.** What does Shane need?

**2.** In what sequence does Carlene tell the location?

    a) _____

    b) _____

    c) _____

**3**. How does Carlene specify which table?

**4.** Circle the kind of relationship they have:

    family      friends      strangers

Answers on p. 157.

## Where Do You Keep It?

On videotape, you will see eight dialogues about where certain objects are kept. After watching each dialogue, write the number of the dialogue in the blank below the illustration of the object discussed. Then write the same number in the location described in the dialogue. We have given the answers for Dialogue 1 as an example.

_____  _____  _____  _____  **1**

Note how the signers negotiate information to confirm or clarify the location. Also note the two ways they begin the conversations:

- giving a reason, then asking the other person to get something
- asking where the person keeps the object

Answers on p. 157.

## How Many Bedrooms Do You Have?

Sign each of the questions below before watching the sign models on videotape. Use the sentence structures taught in class, i.e., yes/no questions and wh-word questions. Then practice by imitating the sign models.

**1.** Ask someone if the house s/he lives in is small or large.

**2.** Ask the number of bedrooms and bathrooms.

**3.** Ask if the living room has a fireplace. If so, ask if it is made of wood, stone or brick.

**4.** Ask if the floor is wood or carpeted.

**5.** Ask if the shower and tub are separate or combined.

**6.** Ask whether the refrigerator, stove, and dishwasher are color coordinated.

**7.** Ask if the person has a garage. If so, ask if it has an automatic or manually opened door.

**8.** Ask if the person's house has a laundry room.

## Rearrangements and Renovations

On videotape, you will see four dialogues in which people discuss how certain rooms were rearranged or renovated, and plans for redesigning a backyard. The following are "Before" and "After" floor plans for the area discussed in each dialogue. After watching each one, fill in the "After" floor plan with the rearranged furniture or added features discussed on the videotape. See following:

**Dialogue 1:** Putting a grand piano in the living room.

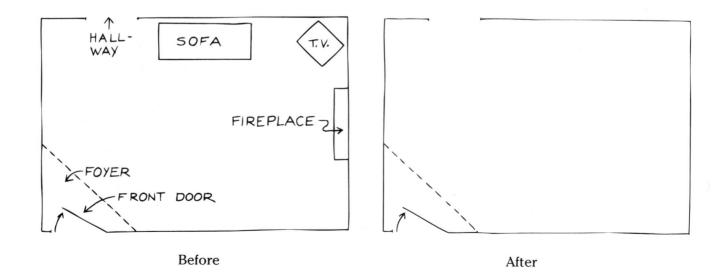

Before                                                    After

**Dialogue 2**: Redesigning the backyard.

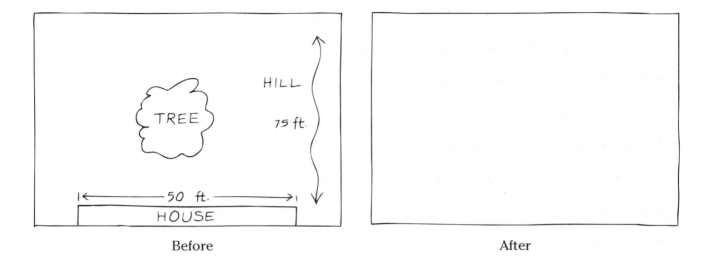

Before                    After

**Dialogue 3**: Fitting a new roommate's things into the bedroom.

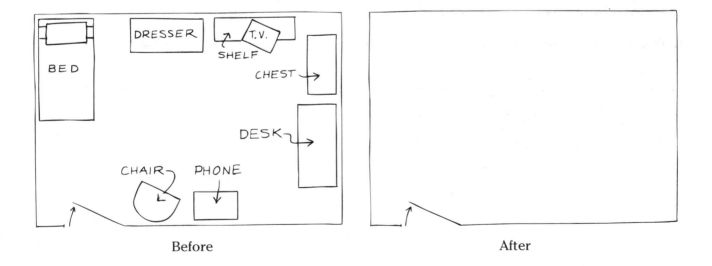

Before                    After

**Dialogue 4**: Remodeling the bathroom.

Before                                                    After

Answers on pp. 157–158.

## Numbers: 101–109 and Counting by Hundreds

On videotape, Malcolm and Ramona demonstrate each of these number forms: 101–109 and hundreds from 100 to 1,000. Pay attention to how they form the numbers. Then practice signing the numbers yourself.

## Number Practice

Watch the videotaped sentences, each of which includes a number. Write down the number signed in each sentence, and the topic to which it refers.

| number | topic | number | topic |
|--------|-------|--------|-------|
| Ex. $200 | cost of decoder for TV | | |
| 1. _____ | _____ | 6. _____ | _____ |
| 2. _____ | _____ | 7. _____ | _____ |
| 3. _____ | _____ | 8. _____ | _____ |
| 4. _____ | _____ | 9. _____ | _____ |
| 5. _____ | _____ | 10. _____ | _____ |

Answers on p. 158.

## Fingerspelling: Double-Letter Words

The sign models on videotape will sign sentences with at least one fingerspelled word. All of the words have double letters. Write the words they spell in the blanks below. Afterwards, rewind and watch the sentences again, this time attending to how the double-letter pattern is produced. Imitate the pattern to practice fluency.

1. _____

2. _____

3. _____

4. _____

5. _____  _____

6. _____

7. _____

8. _____

9. _____

10. _____  _____

Answers on p. 158.

## Where's a Good Place to Shop?

In the videotaped dialogue, Sandra informs her husband, Lon, that Anthony has arrived, then Lon and Anthony discuss home improvements. After watching the dialogue, answer the questions below.

**1.** What has Lon heard about Anthony?

**2.** What does Anthony want from Lon?

**3.** If you had to make a directory of the store, what different sections would you include?

_____  _____  _____

_____  _____  _____

_____  _____  _____

4. On the illustration below, mark the location of the store according to Lon's directions:

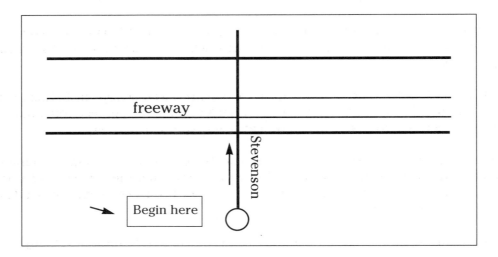

Answers on p. 158.

## Classifiers that Show Plurality

In his description of the various items sold at Home Depot, Lon uses many examples of classifiers that show plurality. There are several ways to indicate plurality in ASL: using cardinal numbers to specify how many (i.e., two, three, four); using quantifier signs to indicate a few, some, or many; or using classifiers.

You can use a specific type of classifier called *plural classifiers* to represent an unspecified number of objects. Or, classifiers that show the location of a noun can be *repeated* to show a plural number of things. Both plural classifiers and repeated classifier signs not only indicate plurality, but also may show the location, shape, or orientation of the objects they represent (i.e., whether they are upright, face down, arranged in rows, etc.).*

Clips from the dialogue are shown again in slow motion. Notice the classifiers Lon uses and watch how he uses them to show how the various items are arranged.

**Example 1**: The classifier in this segment represents stacks of flat or thin objects. Lon uses it for stacks of lumber, but it could also be used for stacks of newspapers, books or plates, piled-up boxes of VCRs, large bags of dog food piled on top of each other, etc. (repeated classifier)

* The English language has classifiers for representing plurality of a noun, for example, a *handful* of marbles, a *bunch* of bananas, a *herd* of cows. A few English classifiers also indicate the arrangement of things the noun represents (i.e., *stacks* of lumber, *rows* of plants) without indicating location.

14

**Example 2**: The classifier in this segment means rows of tall, upright objects. Lon uses the classifier to represent rows of different kinds of moldings, but it could also be used for a row of trees, telephone poles lined up close together, fishing poles lined up against a wall, a pocketful of pens. Signed with palm-down orientation, it could be used for an array of paintbrushes, chopsticks, etc. (plural classifier)

**Example 3**: This is another example of the classifier used in Example 1. This time Lon uses it to represent large bags of cement and stucco, as well as stacks of bricks, rock, or other masonry materials. (repeated classifier)

**Example 4**: The classifier in this segment is used to indicate a wall of objects, in this case a wall of different kinds of paint. It could be also be used for shelves filled with books from floor to ceiling, a wall covered with pictures, rows of cups lining a wall, etc. (plural classifier)

**Examples 5 and 6**: In these two segments Lon represents objects with the same general shape (doors and windows) by using the same classifier; he indicates that they are stacked upright, front to back. This classifier could also be used for books or records on a shelf, videocassettes lined up on a shelf, etc. (repeated classifier)

**Example 7**: This is a classifier for bowl-shaped objects. Lon uses it to represent many models of toilets displayed in a section of the store. (repeated classifier)

**Example 8**: This classifier represents a variety of a certain kind of object in an area. Lon uses it to represent a large selection of different tools. It could also be used for many different foods in a buffet, many different kinds of furniture in a showroom, a variety of art supplies or computer equipment on display, etc. (plural classifier)

# The Story Corner

### "Exploring a Cave"

Cinnie tells a true story about herself and a group of friends taking a trip to explore a cave. How long were they in the cave? Why?

Answers on p. 158.

# LANGUAGE IN PERFORMANCE

## Handshape Stories

Handshape stories are one form of creative play with ASL. In handshape stories all the signs used must be chosen and ordered according to specific rules. There are three kinds of handshape stories: ABC stories, number stories, and one-handshape stories. ABC stories are told using signs in the handshapes of each letter of the manual alphabet, starting with A and ending with Z. This involves using a *pattern* from English, with *signs* from ASL. The ASL signs usually have no relationship to the English letter except for the handshape used. Number stories are similar to ABC stories, but use signs in the handshapes of ASL numbers from 1 to 10, 15, or 20. In one-handshape stories the performer recites a story or poem using only signs in a single handshape.

To appreciate handshape stories, you should first understand how signs are made. Just as spoken languages are made up of different sounds in various combinations, signed languages are made up of certain handshapes that occur in different locations, with various movements and orientations. All signs can be analyzed in terms of these parameters: handshape, movement, location and orientation. As you change any of these parameters, you also change the meaning of the sign. For example, think of the sign for "apple": the X-handshape at the cheek, palm oriented down, and signed with a twisting movement. If you change the *location* of the sign for "apple" to near the eye, the meaning changes to "onion." If you change the *handshape* of the sign for "apple" to the 1-handshape, the meaning changes to a regional sign for "candy." Not all possible handshapes, movements or locations are acceptable in ASL; also, there are ASL handshapes other than those of the letters of the English alphabet. It is the constraint on handshapes—the strict order required—that provides the challenge in creating a handshape story.

**ABC Stories**. The form of ABC stories is traditional, but the stories themselves vary. The most common types are risque, humorous, or horror stories, especially among young people, but they may also relate everyday experiences in a way that entertains and delights the listener. ABC stories may be passed on from one group to another, often with creative alterations or new twists.

On videotape, Dr. Sam Supalla first gives a general introduction to the Language in Performance series. Sam then introduces Ben Bahan, who presents his ABC story "Class Reunion." Because some of the handshapes of the manual alphabet are used in very few ASL signs (for example: E, J, M, P, T), Ben takes advantage of name signs to work these handshapes into his story.* See following page for a list of the handshapes used in the story, followed by the meaning of the sign Ben uses for that handshape.

---

* In many name signs, the first letter of the person's name is signed in particular rule-governed locations. See the Level 1 *Student Workbook*, p. 74, for review. Notice that in this story, Ben does bend the rules by using name signs in direct address. Poetic license is assumed for the strict structure of an ABC story.

| Handshape | Meaning | Handshape | Meaning |
|---|---|---|---|
| A: | "hey there" (informal or intimate sign) | N and O: | "No, I'm wrong." |
| B: | "hello" | P: | correct name sign |
| C: | (handshake) | Q: | "How stupid of me!" |
| D: | "you" | R: | "I didn't realize... |
| E: | name sign | S: | ...how old I'm getting." |
| F: | (looks person over) | T: | name sign of yet another person |
| G: | "You're thin!" | U: | "You were so funny... |
| H and I: | "Hi" to another person | V: | ...as I look back over the years." |
| J: | name sign | W: | "wow" (modified sign) |
| K: | "You're smoking now?" | X: | "Friends... |
| L: | "I'm surprised at you." | Y: | ...are now... |
| M: | another person's name sign | Z: | ...coming from all over." |

**One-Handshape Story**. Sam then introduces Freda Norman, who tells a one-handshape story that illustrates a different form of language play. The objective is to tell a story which is as long as possible without violating any grammar rules, and with appropriate sequencing and organization, while using *only* signs of one handshape. Freda uses the handshape for "5" or "B" which is frequently used in ASL. The story she tells is about a boy, his parents, and the events that occurred throughout the boy's life.

*End of Unit 13*

# Unit 13
## KEY PHRASES

Ask if house has a ceiling fan, ask to describe

Describe bedroom

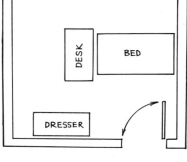

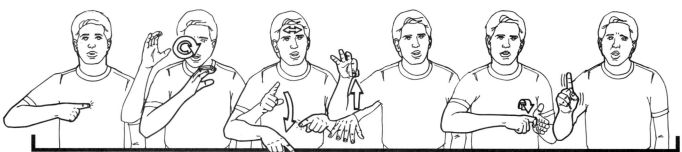

Explain you are looking for a key, ask where

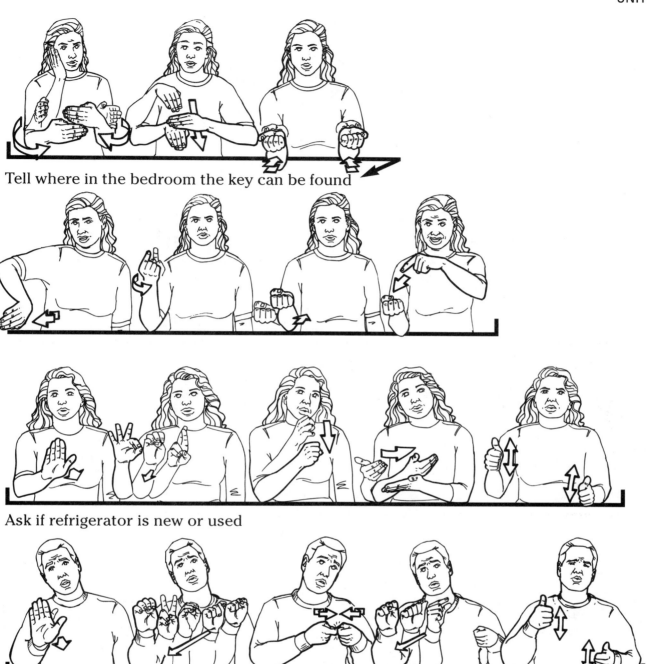

Tell where in the bedroom the key can be found

Ask if refrigerator is new or used

Ask whether stove is electric or gas

# VOCABULARY REVIEW

AROUND THE HOUSE

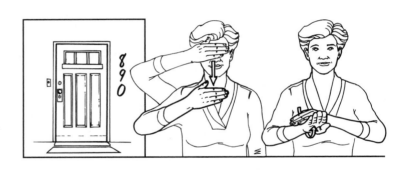

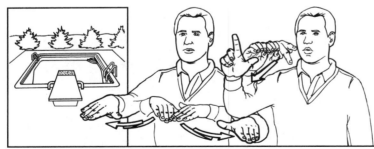

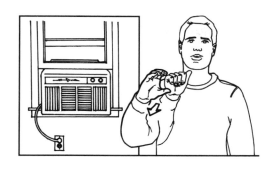 

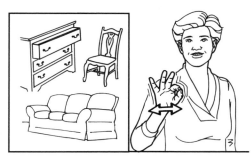

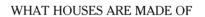

WHAT HOUSES ARE MADE OF

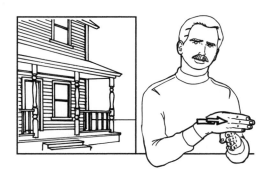

 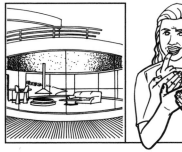 

ROOMS IN THE HOUSE

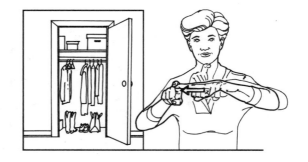

FEATURES OF LIVING ROOM

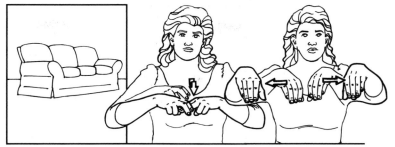

FEATURES OF
KITCHEN

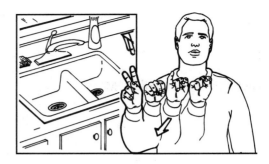

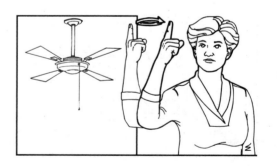

FEATURES OF BEDROOM

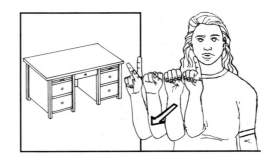

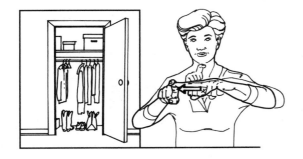

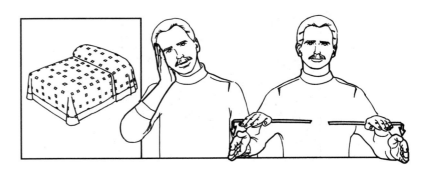

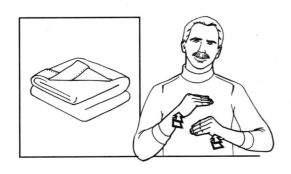

**FEATURES OF BATHROOM**

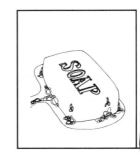

**ACCESSORIES/FIXTURES**

OFFICE OBJECTS

HOME OBJECTS

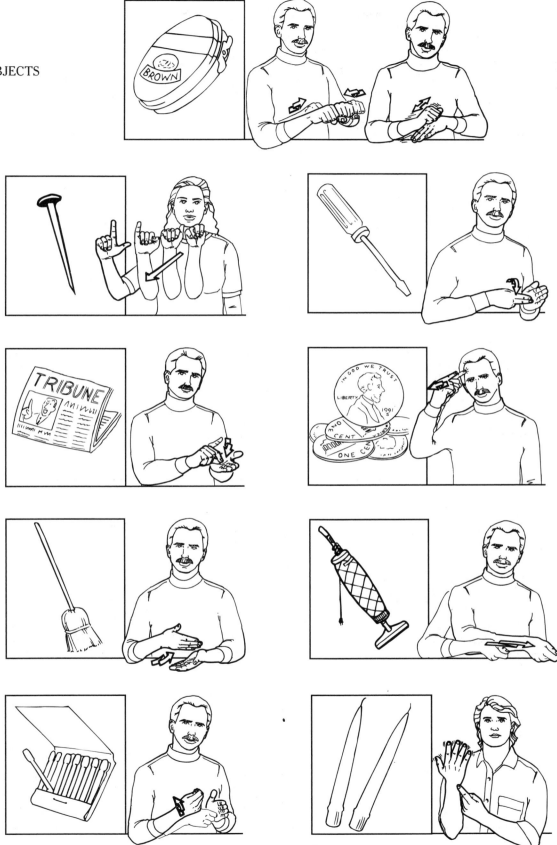

OPINIONS ABOUT PLACES

SIZES OF ROOM/HOUSE

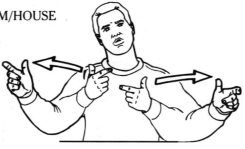  

REARRANGEMENTS
AND RENOVATIONS

*Definition:*
To appear, look, act differently
(functions as a comment or
an opinion)

*Definition:*
To trade in, replace or
exchange (functions as
a verb)

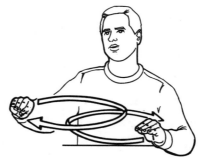

*Definition:*
To move things
around, to re-arrange
(functions as a verb)

*Definition:*
To make improvements,
to update, to look new
(functions as a verb)

*Definition:*
Having nothing in the
space, empty, nothing
there

*Definition:*
To discard, get rid of,
throw away big objects

QUANTIFIERS

All — None

THE LOST
SHOE STORY

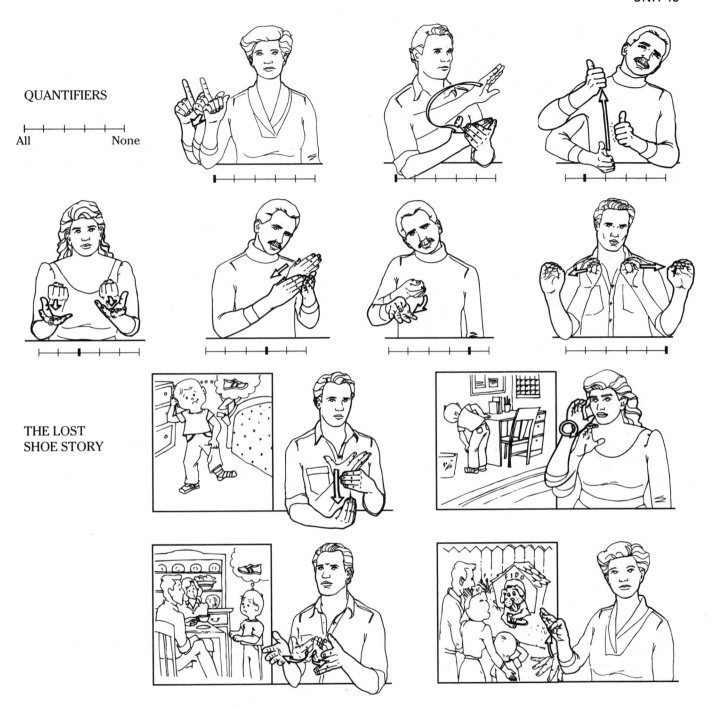

# UNIT 14
# Complaining, Making Suggestions and Requests

## LANGUAGE IN ACTION

### Asking to Borrow a Truck

Read the situation below before watching the videotaped series of conversations, "Asking to Borrow a Truck." Then watch the tape and try to follow the intent of the exchange. Do not concern yourself with unfamiliar signs, but use context to help you figure out the meaning. After you can follow the conversation, fill in the information requested at the end of the exercise.

**Situation:** Anthony has just bought a dresser and needs to borrow a truck to take it home.

(Anthony goes to Joe's home and finds him washing the car.)

*Anthony:* greets Joe
*Joe:* greets Anthony, asks what's happening
*Anthony:* asks if he still has a truck
*Joe:* says yes, tells where it is, asks why
*Anthony:* tells about his purchase, **asks if he can borrow the truck, explains why** he needs it
*Joe:* **responds**
*Anthony:* accepts explanation, says he will ask around
*Anthony:* } leavetakings...
*Joe:*

(Anthony goes to a playing field where his friend Shane is sitting on the bench, waiting for his turn at bat.)

*Anthony:* gets Shane's attention, **makes request**
*Shane:* **responds**, asks why
*Anthony:* explains why
*Shane:* asks if he knows Pat (name sign)
*Anthony:* spells out name to confirm
*Shane:* confirms, explains she has an old truck
*Anthony:* asks if Pat's truck is very old
*Shane:* gives opinion, suggests Anthony go see her and find out
*Anthony:* asks if Pat still lives near the park
*Shane:* replies affirmatively
*Anthony:* says he'll go see her (another ballplayer tells Shane he's up at bat)
*Anthony:* } leavetakings...
*Shane:*

(Anthony approaches Pat, who is mowing the lawn.)

*Anthony:* } greetings
*Pat:*
*Anthony:* asks why her husband is not mowing the lawn
*Pat:* complains about husband
*Anthony:* responds
*Pat:* asks why Anthony is here

35

| Anthony: | **gives reason, makes request** |
| --- | --- |
| Pat: | asks where Anthony lives |
| Anthony: | tells where: nearby, in Berkeley |
| Pat: | tells him that's not really near, it's far |
| Anthony: | disagrees |
| Pat: | **responds to request** |
| Anthony: | tells Pat he will check with other people |
| Pat: | apologizes |
| Anthony: | responds |
| Anthony: Pat: | } leavetakings... |

(Anthony goes to Cinnie's place, and finds her reading the newspaper on her front porch.)

| Anthony: Cinnie: | } greetings |
| --- | --- |
| Anthony: | tells about his purchase, **makes request** |
| Cinnie: | **responds** |
| Anthony: | responds, tells Cinnie he'll get back to her if he cannot find another truck |
| Cinnie: | suggests he check with Lon who is coming by any minute |
| Anthony: | agrees |
| Cinnie: | offers him the paper |
| Anthony: | asks for sports section |
| Cinnie: Anthony: | } discuss their favorite teams |

(Lon arrives.)

| Cinnie: | (gets Anthony's attention) tells him Lon is here |
| --- | --- |
| Anthony: Lon: | } greetings |
| Anthony: | explains situation, **makes request** |
| Lon: | **responds** |
| Anthony: | asks if he can pick it up tomorrow at 3:00 |
| Lon: | agrees |
| Anthony: | expresses relief |
| All: | leavetakings |

Key phrases that express target language functions for this unit are highlighted. Observe how Anthony makes the same request in different ways, and how the reasons given for his request vary in detail with each person he asks. The reason he gives to Joe at the beginning includes information about his purchase and the fact that the store doesn't make deliveries. Giving a reason to Lon at the end, he explains that he tried to borrow a truck from several people to no avail, but Cinnie suggested he contact Lon. Watch the dialogue once more and observe the reasons Anthony gives to each person.

The responses that different people give to Anthony's request also vary. Write down the type of response (see list below), and fill in the explanation or suggestion given by each person.

### types of response

- agree, with condition
- agree, tell shortcoming
- decline, tell why
- decline, suggest other solution
- hedge

|        | type of response | explanation/suggestion |
|--------|------------------|------------------------|
| Joe:   | _____ | _____ |
| Shane: | _____ | _____ |
| Pat:   | _____ | _____ |
| Cinnie: | _____ | _____ |
| Lon:   | _____ | _____ |

Answers on p. 158.

## LANGUAGE IN PRACTICE

G R A M M A R  N O T E S

## Inflections for Temporal Aspect

Some verbs in ASL may be inflected for various purposes, i.e., to show who did what to whom, to show how something is moved from one location to another, or to show manner of movement. Inflections involve a change in the movement of the sign. The type of inflection discussed here is for temporal aspect, and shows the *frequency or duration of action* represented by the verb. If, for example, you want to complain about your health or an on-going personal problem, you would most likely inflect the verb sign to indicate how frequently or how long the problem has occurred.*

If a problem, activity or situation has occurred only once, use the **uninflected** form, which is the basic form of the verb with its basic movement. This is an example of an uninflected verb.

If a problem, activity or situation occurs frequently or regularly (several times a day, every day, every Monday), use **recurring inflection** by signing the verb with several repetitions. This is an illustration of the same verb signed with recurring inflection.

If a problem, activity or situation has occurred continuously with little interruption (for the whole hour, all morning, all week long), use **continuous inflection** by signing the verb with a repeated circular movement. This illustration shows the same verb signed with continuous inflection.

*Not all verbs can be inflected. Many of the verbs in the category "Complaints about ...." in the Vocabulary Review section at the end of this unit are examples of temporal aspect inflections.

37

## Demonstration

On videotape, you will see the following three verb forms demonstrated:

- uninflected form (Cinnie)
- recurring inflection (Mary)
- continuous inflection (Priscilla)

Note how the time signs in each sentence agree with the inflections.

Next on the videotape, you will see 18 sentences, each with an uninflected or inflected form of the verb sign indicating how often the activity has occurred. Circle which verb form is used in each sentence. Also note how the time signs agree with the inflections.

1.   uninflected       recurring       continuous

2.   uninflected       recurring       continuous

3.   uninflected       recurring       continuous

4.   uninflected       recurring       continuous

5.   uninflected       recurring       continuous

6.   uninflected       recurring       continuous

7.   uninflected       recurring       continuous

8.   uninflected       recurring       continuous

9.   uninflected       recurring       continuous

10.   uninflected       recurring       continuous

11.   uninflected       recurring       continuous

12.   uninflected       recurring       continuous

13.   uninflected       recurring       continuous

14.   uninflected       recurring       continuous

15.   uninflected       recurring       continuous

16.   uninflected       recurring       continuous

17.   uninflected       recurring       continuous

18.   uninflected       recurring       continuous

Answers on p. 158.

# Spatial Agreement

**Talking About a Third Person**. When you talk about a third person, it is important that you use your signing space, verb inflections and pronouns appropriately. (By a "third person" we mean someone other than yourself, the "first person," and the person with whom you're talking, the "second person.") The third person can be present and in view, or out of sight, whereabouts known or unknown. The important thing is to *set up the referent for the third person in a certain location, and then use pronouns and inflections on verbs that agree with that location.*

> **Talking about a third person who is present:** When you talk about someone who is present in the room, refer to that person's actual location. If that person moves to another location in the room, refer to the new location to talk about that person.
>
> What if someone was present and then left the room? Usually a new location is established in the direction in which the person was last seen: if s/he went out the front door, point to the direction of the door. If you don't know where the person went, use the location previously established for that person.
>
> **Talking about a third person who is not present:** When you talk about someone who is *not* present in the room, you need to establish a particular location to refer to that person.* You and the person you are talking with should refer to the same location for subsequent references to that third person.

**Using Agreement Verbs.** One verb type in ASL is called **agreement verbs**.** These verbs are inflected to show who did what to whom by incorporating the subject (the person doing the action) and the object (the person receiving the action) in the movement of the sign. The movement *agrees with* the locations established for the pronouns. (Sometimes the palm orientation rather than the movement of the verb indicates the subject and object, for example, in the sign for "look at.") When using agreement verbs, begin the movement of the verb sign near the location of the subject, and end the movement near the location of the object. See the illustration below showing how the movement path of the verb changes to agree with different pronouns.

(you to third person)    (third person to you)    (you to third person)    (third person to you)

> **Using Pronouns with Plain Verbs.** What if you want to talk about a third person but the verbs you use are not the type that can change movement or orientation to reflect the subject and object? (These verbs are called plain verbs—see the Level 1 *Student Workbook*, p. 55.) You must use pronouns with these verbs to specify the subject and object. As discussed previously, using personal pronouns in ASL involves pointing to certain locations. Where you point needs to be consistent within a conversation, and follow the guidelines discussed above.

*A general rule for establishing locations to represent non-present persons is: if you refer to one person, designate a location on your dominant side; if you refer to two persons, designate a location for the first person on your non-dominant side, then a different location for the second person on your dominant side.

**This is a revised term for the type we called "inflecting verbs" in Unit 9 of the Level 1 *Student Workbook*, p. 108. We use this term based on Carol Padden's paper "The Relation Between Space and Grammar in ASL Verb Morphology" in *Sign Language Research: Theoretical Issues* (Ceil Lucas, ed.), Gallaudet Univ. Press, Washington D.C., 1990. Many of the verbs illustrated in the "Making Request" category of the Vocabulary Review at the end of this unit are agreement verbs.

## Demonstration

Watch the four scenes on videotape. In each scene, when one signer refers to a third person (either present or not present), you will see an arrow pointing to the location established for that person. Then one signer will refer to the third person in the wrong location. You will see another arrow that does *not* correspond to the first arrow. At this point, the scene is frozen. The dialogue resumes with the signer repeating the last sentence, this time using the correct movement and/or location. You will then see an arrow that agrees with the location designated earlier.

**Scene 1:** Third person is present
Mary asks Anthony to ask Pat for a key. Pat is sitting in the background. Pay attention to how Mary refers to Pat.

**Scene 2:** Third person is not present (but is associated with a certain place)
Shane asks Carlene where Michelle is. Carlene points in the direction of Michelle's office. Pay attention to how Shane refers to Michelle.

**Scene 3:** Third person is not present
Cinnie tells Dan about her aunt Maureen. Pay attention to how Cinnie refers to Maureen throughout the conversation.

**Scene 4**: Third person was present, but is now out of sight
Sandra asks Pat to give a letter to David (the young man who just left). Pay attention to how Sandra refers to David.


## CONVERSATION PRACTICE

To practice referring to a third person using agreement verbs, find a partner and role play the situations below.

---

**Situation 1:** Third person is present
Pretend there is another person in the room besides you and your partner. Ask your partner if s/he has any aspirin. Your partner should suggest you ask the other person in the room. Explain that you have a headache, and ask if your partner would go ask the other person for aspirin.

**Situation 2:** Third person is not present (but is associated with a certain place)
Imagine you are in a workplace with several offices in your immediate environment. You and your partner are talking when you are interrupted by a phone call. The call is for someone named Terry, but you don't know who that is. When you ask your partner where Terry is, s/he should reply by pointing to Terry's office. Ask your partner if s/he'd mind telling Terry there is a phone call for her.

**Situation 3:** Third person is not present
Tell your partner something s/he doesn't know about a mutual friend (or a famous person).

**Situation 4:** Third person was present, but is now out of sight
You're talking with your partner. Pretend that another person comes in to ask you a question, and leaves in another direction. Now, ask your partner who that person was. When s/he says the name you realize *that's* the person for whom a package arrived today. Since you are in a hurry, ask your partner to tell that person about the package.

---

# Making Requests

In the four videotaped dialogues, notice how the signers use agreement verbs and pronouns. Then, after watching each dialogue, fill in the information requested below.

**Dialogue 1**

    **1.** What did Tina Jo ask Cinnie to do?

    **2.** What was her reason for the request?

    **3.** Why did Cinnie hesitate?

    **4.** What did they agree on?

Notice how Tina Jo points to a location on her right to refer to the pharmacy, and how Cinnie uses the same location for subsequent references.

**Dialogue 2**

    **1.** What did Carlene ask Lon?

    **2.** What was Lon's response?

    **3.** Why did Carlene say it wasn't a good idea?

    **4.** What did they agree on?

Notice how Carlene points to her left to refer to her parents-in-law, then how Lon points to his right to refer to his friend.

**Dialogue 3**

    **1.** What did the caller want?

    **2.** What was Anthony's response?

    **3.** What did Anthony suggest?

    **4.** What did they finally agree on?

Notice that Sandra and Anthony refer to the location of the phone to indicate the caller.

**Dialogue 4**

    **1.** Why did Lon want to see Pat?

    **2.** Why wasn't Priscilla able to catch Pat?

    **3.** What did Lon ask Priscilla to do next?

Notice how Priscilla refers to Pat by pointing to where she was last seen:
- She points to the door Pat went out.
- Later she indicates the direction in which Pat drove off.

UNIT 14

Answers on p. 159.
## Clock Numbers

Watch Steve's demonstration of the following clock number forms on videotape.

| | |
|---|---|
| 9:04 | 7:48 |
| 5:23 | 4:14 |
| 1:11 | 6:59 |
| 10:35 | 12:27 |
| 11:03 | 8:16 |

Practice signing the numbers. Make sure you use a short pause between the hour and minute numbers.

## Clock Numbers Practice

On screen, you will see eight sentences signed by several people. Write down the clock number(s) and the topic given in each sentence. There may be more than one number, so pay close attention.

number(s)        topic

1. _____  _____

2. _____  _____

3. _____  _____

4. _____  _____

5. _____  _____

6. _____  _____

7. _____  _____

8. _____  _____

Answers on p. 159.

## Fingerspelling: Common Fingerspelled Words

Watch the ten sentences on videotape. Write down only the words that are fingerspelled in each sentence. Be sure to notice *all* the fingerspelled words: fill in each of the blanks below.

1. _____, _____

2. _____, _____

3. _____, _____

4. _____, _____

5. _____, _____

6. _____, _____, _____

7. _____, _____, _____

8. _____, _____, _____

9. _____, _____, _____

10. _____, _____, _____, _____

Answers on p. 159.

## The Fortune Teller

The fortune teller gladly gives advice, but only about problems with pets, family, roommates or neighbors. Write down each person's complaint, the advice given, and the person's reaction to the advice.

*Mary's complaint:* _____

*Advice:* _____

*Reaction:* _____

*Anthony's complaint:* _____

*Advice:* _____

*Reaction:* _____

*Dan's complaint:* _____

*First advice:* _____

*Second advice:* _____

*Reaction:* _____

Why do you think the fortune teller didn't give appropriate advice to Dan?

*Bonus:* What did the fortune teller say at the very end?

Answers on p. 159.

# The Story Corner

## "Final Exam"

Ben tells an anecdote about a student taking a final exam for a math class. How did the student outwit the professor?

Answer on p. 159.

# LANGUAGE IN PERFORMANCE

## Cheers and Songs

Many people assume that Deaf people do not have music in their lives. Although Deaf people may not experience music the same way you do, they can enjoy the rhythmic pleasures associated with it. In ASL, rhythmic images are created by the skillful selection and arrangement of signs presented with varied movements—soft, staccato, prolonged, flowing—to render music visually.

**Cheers.** On videotape, Sam Supalla talks about Deaf children's enjoyment of visual rhythms in school cheers performed at sporting events. Freda Norman gives one example of a halftime cheer she remembers from basketball games at the Virginia School for the Deaf (VSD). Notice how the signs selected fit the distinctive beat commonly used in signed cheers: one, two, one-two-three.

**Songs.** Sam goes on to explain that a few songs have been translated into ASL, and then passed on until their form has become traditional. These songs may be part of the entertainment presented at events both at schools for the Deaf and in the Deaf community at large. Songs have been performed at homecoming games, Literary Society meetings, and graduation ceremonies, as well as at formal openings of conventions. Themes may range from group spirit and solidarity to romance or patriotism, although lyrics that have a clear story line are most easily adapted into ASL. Styles and rhythms are also diverse, from formal and stately to visual renditions of rap music. Sometimes songs are performed with auditory accompaniment for hearing members of an audience, but Deaf people usually prefer songs presented only in Sign, using the visual rhythms that fit the constraints of ASL rather than the rhythms of sound.*

Ella Lentz presents a well-known American song that has been adapted into ASL. As Sam asks, can you guess what it is?

Answer on p. 159.

*End of Unit 14*

---

*This may be one reason that interpreted music is more popular among a hearing or hard-of-hearing audience than it is among Deaf people. Interpreters often try to follow the auditory rhythm, which may not fit an artistic translation into ASL.

# Unit 14
## KEY PHRASES

MAKING SUGGESTIONS ABOUT HEALTH

Tell about itching all over after every bath

Make suggestion (phrase 1)

Make suggestion (phrase 2)

Make suggestion (phrase 3)

COMPLAIN ABOUT OTHERS

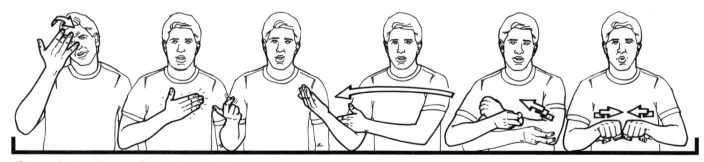

Complain about dog taking shoes

Complain about children horsing around too much

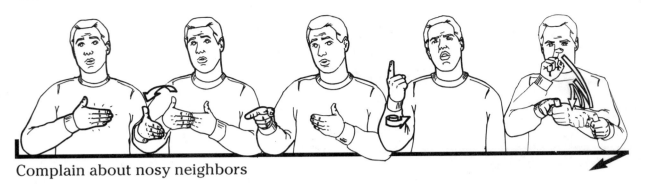

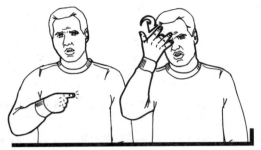

Complain about nosy neighbors

## MAKING REQUESTS

Request help with task (pick up a prescription from store)

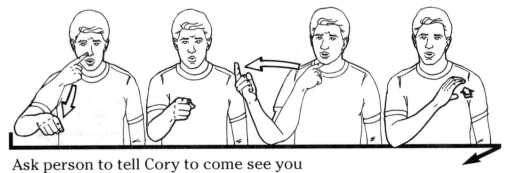

Ask person to tell Cory to come see you

Ask permission to join a group

Request person to hold your chair for you

Request to move up time of meeting to eleven a.m.

Decline, suggest alternative time (next day)

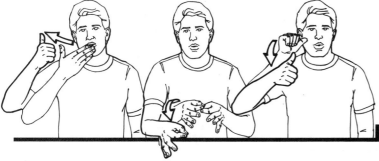

ASKING TO BORROW A TRUCK

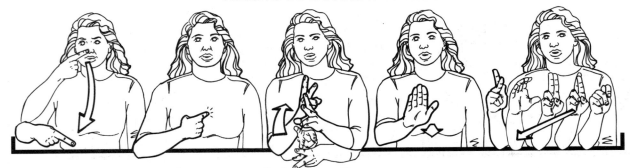

Request permission to borrow truck (phrase 1)

Request permission to borrow truck (phrase 2)

Request permission to borrow truck (phrase 3)

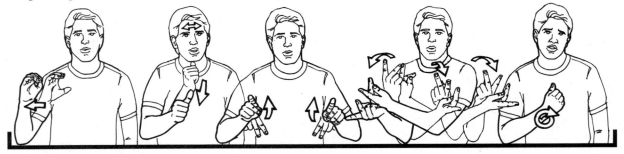

Decline, tell why (truck owned by company)

Decline, tell why (brother has it)

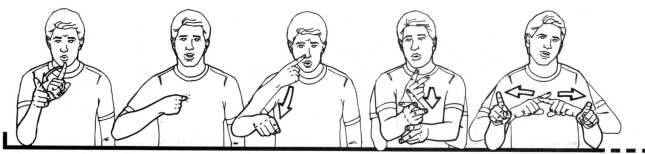

Hedge, explain you don't mind, but...

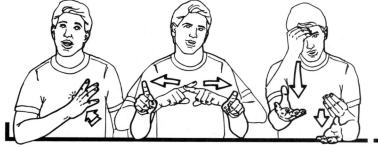

Agree, explain shortcoming

Agree with condition (that person put in more gas)

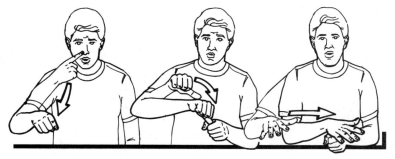

# VOCABULARY REVIEW

AILMENTS

51

TELL YOU DON'T FEEL GOOD

EMPATHIZE

 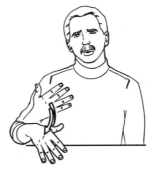 

REMEDIES

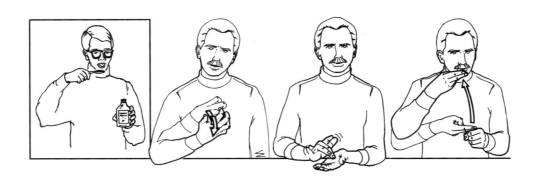

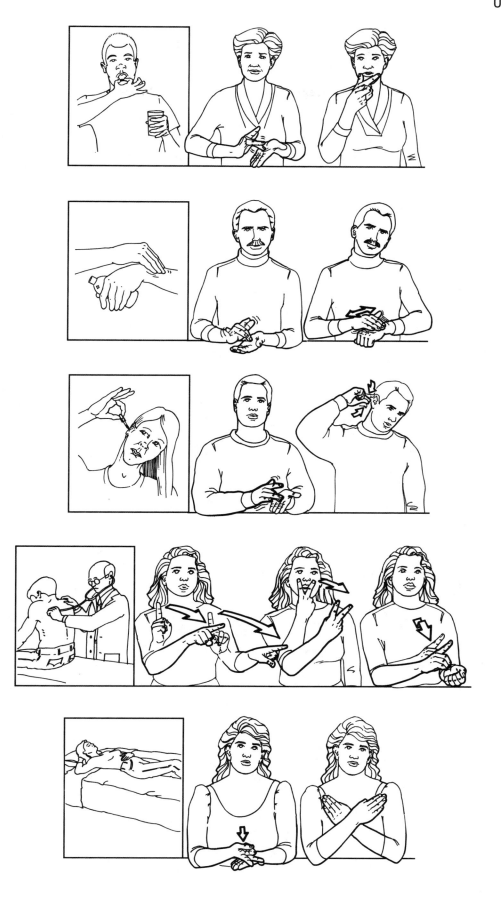

TIME SIGNS:
Recurring

TIME SIGNS:
Continuous

PET'S BEHAVIORS THAT
CAN BE IRRITATING

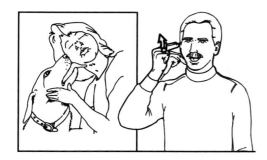

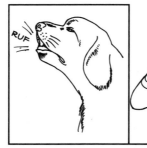

CHILDREN'S BEHAVIORS THAT
CAN BE IRRITATING

55

ROOMMATE/SPOUSE'S
BEHAVIORS THAT
CAN BE IRRITATING

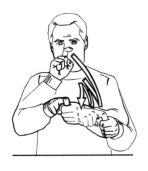

NEIGHBOR'S BEHAVIORS THAT
CAN BE IRRITATING

AGREEMENT VERBS*

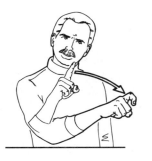

\* These verbs are modified according to locations of the object and the subject. See GRAMMAR NOTES, "Spatial Agreement" on page 39 of the *Student Workbook–Level 2*.

# UNIT 15
# Exchanging Personal Information: Life Events

## LANGUAGE IN ACTION

### Discussing Nationalities

Read the situation below before watching the videotaped conversation "Discussing Nationalities." Then watch the tape and try to follow the intent of the exchange. Do not concern yourself with unfamiliar signs, but use context to help you figure out the meaning. After you are able to understand the conversation, fill in the information requested throughout the dialogue below.

**Situation:** Tina Jo, Cinnie and Mary chat outside on a balcony at a pool party. When Cinnie leaves to get drinks, the conversation turns to discussing her nationality.

Cinnie: offers to get drinks for the others

Tina Jo: ⎫
Mary: ⎬ respond

Cinnie: says that she'll be back

Tina Jo: **asks** Mary what Cinnie's **maiden name** is

Mary: gives name: Nettum

Tina Jo: **asks what nationality the name is**

Mary: **tells nationalities** of Cinnie's parents

[fill in father's nationality] _____

[fill in mother's nationality] _____

Tina Jo: **asks the origin** of Cinnie's husband's name (Brennan)

Mary: **gives information** [origin of husband's name] _____

Tina Jo: **comments**

Cinnie: (returns with drinks)

Mary: (to Cinnie) checks information about Cinnie's parents

Cinnie: confirms

Tina Jo: explains **what she thought Cinnie's nationality was** [fill in nationality] _____

Cinnie: comments that others have thought the same thing, asks about Tina Jo's nationality

Tina Jo: **gives information**

[fill in mother's nationality] _____

[fill in father's nationality] _____

Cinnie: responds

Answers on p. 160.

**Key phrases** that express target language functions for this unit are highlighted. Replay the conversation and rehearse the key phrases.

# LANGUAGE IN PRACTICE

## Narrating About Life Events

Narratives usually include three main parts: an *introduction* that tells the topic, gives necessary background, or creates a context for the information to follow; a *main body* which may include one event or a series of events; a *closing* such as a summary or evaluation. In this unit, the narratives about people's life events tend to begin with information on where someone was born and raised. Then the life events are sequenced in chronological order, ending with a statement of the person's current situation or future plans.

## Transitions Between Events

Throughout the body of these narratives, signers use different transitions to signal the end of one event and the beginning of the next. Clear transitions help the listener follow the sequence of events. Varying the transitions is one way to make the story interesting, as each kind of transition provides a different focus for the event that follows.

**1) Pauses:** This is the most common transition. At the end of an event lower your head slightly, pause your signing, then raise your head to signal the beginning of the next event. You will see many examples of this transition on tape.

**2) When clauses**: Another transition used between events is a "when clause." Sentences with when clauses have two parts: the when clause itself is always at the beginning, and includes raised eyebrows and a head tilt; in the second part of the sentence the eyebrows and head go back to a neutral position while telling the event. You can use a when clause to tell about events in three ways:

- by telling someone's *age* when the event took place ("when I was four, I started kindergarten")
- by mentioning another *event* that preceded it ("right after graduation, I got married")
- by telling the *year* the event occurred ("in 1985, he passed away")

**3) Time signs indicating a period of time:** The sign illustrated here is frequently used to indicate that an unspecified period of time elapsed between events. The sign form can be changed or non-manual behaviors can be added to show the relative length of time: use "cs" with this sign to indicate "shortly afterwards," "mm" for "a while later," and "open mouth" to mean "a long time later."

This sign can also be used in conjunction with specific time signs, for example to indicate "five years later" or "after three months."

Specific time signs can also be used alone to tell the time period between events. Signed with raised eyebrows, this signals the beginning of the next event.

## Demonstration

In this segment of the videotape Ethan demonstrates the following transitions. These are clips from his narrative "Jose's Life Story." The clips are shown in slow motion so that you can see the non-manual behaviors that occur with a when clause and with time signs:

1. when clause used with age
2. when clause used with another event
3. when clause used with year
4. when clause used with age
5. when clause used with age
6. time sign — unspecified
7. time sign — specific

# Jose's Life Story

Now watch Ethan narrate "Jose's Life Story," paying particular attention to the transitions he uses between events. Below is a picture sequence of Jose's life to help you follow the narrative.

# Cinnie's Autobiography

Watch how Cinnie talks about her life, beginning with her birth and ending with her future plans. Then replay the story and fill in the outline below.

<u>events</u>                                       <u>information given</u>

**Introduction**
    birth          _____

    family         _____

**Main Body**
    school         _____

   first college    _____

 second college     _____

Peace Corps
  assignment       _____

travels after
the Peace Corps    _____

                 _____

first job back
  in the U.S.       _____

   wedding         _____

jobs in California   _____

                 _____

                 _____

graduate school        _____

husband's career change    _____

**Closing**
current plans        _____

_____

Answers on p. 160.

**Transitions.** Review the first portion of the story, from her birth until she goes into the Peace Corps (time code 00:00 to 1:38): watch how she uses when clauses with age and events. Notice also how she uses the time sign illustrated here to indicate periods of time that elapsed between events.

Now watch the portion of the story about her world travels (time code 1:50 to 2:37). Cinnie uses the sign illustrated here in two ways: once to say that she completed her stint in the Peace Corps, and also to signal the end of one event and the beginning of another. A good example of this second use of the sign is when she talks about traveling with her boyfriend. Play this segment of her story again and observe how she uses the sign to sequence a series of stops on her trip.

Throughout her story Cinnie uses both specific time signs (i.e., for spring of 1979, last year, this summer) as well as time signs that tell a period of time (i.e., for six months) as a way to mark transitions between major events. Replay the narrative and observe how she uses specific time signs with non-manual behaviors to make her transitions clear.

## Notes on the Narrative

**Cinnie's college experiences.** As you may recall from the "Brief History of Deaf America" reading in the Level 1 *Student Workbook,* Gallaudet University, founded in 1864, is the only liberal arts university in the world established specifically for Deaf students. In 1968, the National Technical Institute for the Deaf (NTID) was founded to provide technical and professional training to Deaf students. Certain colleges around the country were also given funding to establish programs for services to Deaf students. In 1976 Section 504 of the Rehabilitation Act was signed into law, mandating certain standards of accessibility for Deaf and disabled people in any institution receiving federal funds. Deaf students were then able to attend many hearing colleges with interpreting services provided by each college or university. Although many Deaf students do attend hearing colleges around the country, there is still an overwhelming preference for the rich tradition, fellowship and ease of communication that exist at Gallaudet.

**Cinnie's work with the Peace Corps.** People who volunteer for the Peace Corps apply to the type of program they want to work in, such as Health, Forestry or Deaf Education. The Peace Corps sends volunteers to approximately 60 countries; by far the largest number work in health programs. Only a handful of countries have Peace Corps–sponsored Deaf Education programs: the Philippines, Ecuador, Morocco, Haiti, Nepal and Sri Lanka. The Philippines has the largest program, and the only one with a training component. Most volunteers teach in schools for the Deaf, and train local teachers to do the same.

There are over 100 spoken languages used throughout the Philippines. Education for hearing students, however, is primarily in English. In schools for the Deaf, teachers tend to sign a "pidgin" or mix of the native Philippine Sign Language, American Sign Language and English-based sign systems.

**Cinnie's job in Connecticut.** The American School for the Deaf (ASD), founded in 1817 in Hartford, Connecticut by Thomas Gallaudet and Laurent Clerc, was the first public school for the Deaf in the United States. Gallaudet had visited the National Royal Institution for the Deaf in Paris, and invited Clerc, a much-loved Deaf teacher there, to accompany him back to America to establish the first school using ASL as the language of instruction. It was not long before other states established their own schools. Graduates of ASD were recruited to teach in these institutions.

For many years there was at least one residential school for the Deaf in almost every state in the U.S. Residential schools have long been a mainstay of the Deaf community, a place where language, cultural traditions and values are passed from one generation to the next.

**Cinnie's work with Deaf-Blind people.** Among Deaf-Blind people, the largest group is those who are Deaf first and lose their vision later. Many of these people have Usher's Syndrome: congenital deafness with progressive loss of vision from retinitis pigmentosa (tunnel vision and night-blindness). Deaf people can also have other kinds of vision problems, but if ASL is their first language, they will continue to use ASL by following signs in various ways. People who have low vision may need to watch signs from close up; if their visual field is very narrow they may watch signs from a greater-than-normal distance; others may track signs by holding the signer's wrists. People with less or no vision may follow signs tactually by placing their hands over the signer's hands. Certain adaptations in the language are helpful for tactile communication, for example, adding signs for information conveyed through non-manual behaviors. (A person who is blind first and becomes deaf later may prefer to communicate in English, by having English words fingerspelled into his/her palm, or placing his/her hand over the fingerspeller's.)

Although most services to Deaf-Blind people have historically been provided by agencies serving the blind, many Deaf individuals also have been involved in the Deaf-Blind community. Some Deaf people have teaching jobs like Cinnie's, or work as interpreters in the classroom, at conferences or other events.

# Telling About Unexpected Changes

You may have noticed this sign throughout Cinnie's Autobiography and once in Jose's Life Story. The sign is used as a conjunction when telling about an unexpected change that occurs suddenly or without warning.

You will see four minidialogues on videotape in which one person explains to another how plans went awry. In each example, the sign illustrated here is used when telling about the unexpected change in plans. After watching each dialogue, fill in the information requested below.

**Situation 1:** Ethan tells Sandra he thought she had moved away. Sandra explains...

*What happened:* _____

_____

**Situation 2:** Lon asks Malcolm why Tom isn't here. Malcolm explains...

*What happened:* _____

_____

**Situation 3:** Cinnie asks Carlene why George (name sign G-on-chest) has a cast on his leg. Carlene explains...

*What happened:* _____

_____

**Situation 4:** Dan asks why Mary is late. Mary explains...

*What happened:* _____

_____

Answers on p. 160.

Now go back to "Jose's Life Story" and "Cinnie's Autobiography" to see when and how the narrators use this conjunction in their stories to tell about unexpected changes.

# The Immigrants

On screen, Steve describes his family history, including the events that led one side of the family to immigrate to America. Use the diagram of his family tree below to help you follow the narrative.

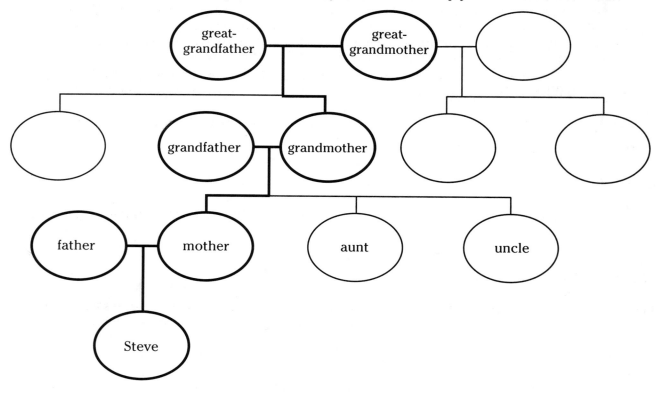

After you understand the sequence of events, fill in the identity of each person described below.

**1.** Nationality is Italian. Went to South Africa on business and was never seen again.

     Identity: _____

**2.** Born in North Carolina of German/Scottish ancestry. After World War II, he moved to California for work, and four years later got married.

     Identity: _____

**3.** Grew up in California and married a man from Yugoslavia. Had three children.

     Identity: _____

**4.** Lived in Yugoslavia, but when the country suffered economic depression and war, decided to move to America with her two kids. Ended up in California, where she met her second husband.

     Identity: _____

Answers on p. 161.

**Telling family history.** In talking about several generations of a family, three language tools are important for keeping the information clear and easy to follow:

- possessive pronouns: This reflects an imaginary family tree and helps keep clear which generation you are referring to.
- listing: You can use the fingers of your weak hand to represent one generation of children or siblings; once you establish which family member a finger represents, you can simply point to the finger to refer to that family member. (Remember that you cannot use your fingers to refer to different generations or different sides of the family at the same time, i.e., you cannot refer to your aunt and your cousins within the same "list.")
- contrastive structure: You can represent one side of the family on your right and other on your left, then refer to the left or right to make clear which side of the family you mean.

Now replay the segment and watch how Steve uses possessive pronouns, listing and contrastive structure to make the narrative clear.

## Numbers: 110–119

Watch Steve sign the numbers 110–119 on videotape. Then practice signing these numbers yourself.

## Number Practice

On screen, you will see ten sentences signed by various people. Each sentence includes a number from 110–119. Write down the number signed in each sentence, and the topic to which it refers.

number                topic

1. _____  _____
2. _____  _____
3. _____  _____
4. _____  _____
5. _____  _____
6. _____  _____
7. _____  _____
8. _____  _____
9. _____  _____
10. _____  _____

Answers on p. 161.

## Dates and Addresses

The next segment of the videotape is divided into four parts in which signers give dates, years, or addresses. Within each of the first three parts, the dates or years are given in random order. Find the appropriate blank below and write in the dates or years given. For the last part, write down the addresses and zip code in the order signed on the videotape.

**Specific Dates**

Date first Deaf president of
Gallaudet University selected    _____

Laurent Clerc's birthdate    _____

Douglas Tilden's birthdate    _____

Founding of the American
School for the Deaf    _____

**Periods of Time**

Wave of immigration to America
from northern Europe    _____

Era of Deaf performers in silent films    _____

Years that captioned films
were popular    _____

Boom of Deaf workers
in the war industry    _____

**Span of Years (from _____ to _____ )**

Life of Laura Searing    _____–_____

Years Germany was divided
into East and West    _____–_____

Years Edward M. Gallaudet served
as college president    _____–_____

The building of the
Golden Gate Bridge    _____–_____

**Addresses**

_____

_____

_____

_____

Answers on p. 161.

# A Show of Hands

"Mark Harrison" and "Liz Svetla" appear as contestants on the game show, "A Show of Hands: Places in the World." The host of the show, "Jacqueline Norris" or "Jacqu," begins by interviewing each contestant. Watch the whole segment, then go back and watch it again to answer the following questions.

**1.** What information did the contestants give about themselves?

Mark: _____

_____

Liz: _____

_____

**2.** What was the first question of the game?

_____

**3.** What was the correct answer given by Mark?

_____

**4.** What was the question about Abbe de l'Epeé?

_____

**5.** What answer did Liz give?

_____

**6.** For the next question, name three countries whose signed names use the I-handshape, what countries did Mark name?

_____

**7.** For the next question, name four countries whose names include the letter Z, what countries did Liz name?

_____

**8.** For the next question, name six countries that do not border an ocean, what four countries did Mark get right?

_____

**9.** Which country did Mark get wrong?

_____

**10.** Name the two other countries that Liz guessed right.

_____

**11.** What prizes were awarded the loser?

_____

**12.** What prize was awarded the winner?

_____

**13.** Who did Liz have in mind to go with her on the trip?

_____

Answers on p. 161.

## It's a Small World

When members of the Deaf community first meet, they often try to figure out what community ties they have in common.* They may try to identify mutual friends and acquaintances, refer to common experiences, shared interests or knowledge. Watch the next video segment in which Yolanda introduces Pat and Priscilla to each other when they meet at a Deaf club. Then answer the following questions:

**1.** How does Yolanda know Pat?

_____

**2.** Is Pat still working?

_____

**3.** How does Yolanda know Priscilla?

_____

**4.** Where is Priscilla from?

_____

**5.** Why does Priscilla think Pat might be related to Clyde?

_____

*For review, read "Meeting Others" and "Maintaining Continuity in Relationships" in the Level 1 _Student Workbook_, pp. 73 and 171.

**6.** Where did Pat grow up?

_____

**7.** Which brother is older, Clyde's father or Pat's father?

_____

**8.** Did all three brothers graduate from the California School for the Deaf at Berkeley?

_____

**9.** Why did Clyde's father move to Ohio during World War I?

_____

**10.** Who has three Deaf daughters and where did they go to college?

_____

**11.** How does Priscilla know the Stecker sisters?

_____

**12.** What does Pat say about the third brother and his daughter?

_____

**13.** What kind of school does the deaf grandson go to?

_____

**14.** What pleased Pat about the grandson's relatives?

_____

**15.** Why does Shane interrupt the conversation?

_____

Answers on p. 161.

Now watch the conversation again, noticing how Priscilla elicits information that helps her make connections between herself and Pat. For example:

- Priscilla asks Pat if she's related to Clyde in Ohio who has the same last name.
- She asks if Pat grew up in Ohio to see if they know other people in common.
- She asks for the three nieces' last name to see if she knows them from Gallaudet.

Also notice how Priscilla checks on other possible connections by following up on other Deaf people in Pat's family. For example:

- She asks what happened to the third brother.
- She asks if the grandson is attending a residential school for the Deaf.

## Notes on the Conversation

**The role of houseparents.** In the dialogue, Pat used to be Yolanda's houseparent (some schools call the position "dorm counselor"). Houseparents have a significant role in the lives of Deaf children at residential schools. They supervise students' activities outside the classroom, including intramural sports and trips off campus. They take on many parenting responsibilities, such as seeing that they do their homework, sending them to the infirmary when they get sick, seeing them off to bed and waking them up in the morning. Remember that most Deaf children have hearing parents. Students fortunate enough to have houseparents fluent in ASL benefit greatly from their guidance. Houseparents with a positive attitude toward signing and Deaf people can be excellent role models, and can instill students with pride and self-esteem. Students not only learn social skills from these houseparents, but also stories, traditions and cultural values.

## The Story Corner

### "The Dead Dog"

Freda tells a story about the efforts of airline personnel to find a missing dog. What was the owner's reaction when she came to pick up the dog? Why did she react that way?

_____

_____

Answers on p. 161.

# LANGUAGE IN PERFORMANCE

## Poetry

Once people become aware of their language as a literary form, they give new attention to how to say things. While there is a long tradition of poetry performed in Sign, early poems were often translations or adaptations of works in English. Then in the late 1960s and early 1970s, with the recognition by linguists of ASL as a rich language distinct from English, ASL poetry flourished.

Poetry stretches the limits of a language—the rules of the language must be understood before they can be violated or exploited for poetic purposes. This creative renaissance that coincided with the linguistic awareness of ASL has allowed Deaf poets to explore the creative possibilities unique to a visual-spatial language. As Sam Supalla says in his introduction, ASL poetry is a vibrant blend of imagery, rhythm, feelings and insight.

### "To a Hearing Mother" by Ella Mae Lentz

Sam introduces Ella's poem by explaining the deep-felt concern Deaf people have about the well-being of Deaf children. Approximately 90% of Deaf children have hearing parents. These parents have the responsibility of deciding what is best for their children, but they usually lack the experience to make such decisions. They may not have access to the Deaf community for guidance and insight, and instead are given advice by hearing professionals, who also lack first-hand experience of what it means to be Deaf.

The tension between the hearing mother and the Deaf community is artistically developed to a poignant resolution. Ella evokes the tension by using space not only to represent the hearing mother and the Deaf people, but also to draw attention to the differences between them in experience, values, and world view. She reasons that both have a role to play in the child's life, for without Deaf people the child would wither and be left with no soul, no sense of self. But without the hearing mothers there would be no more children, and the great people and language would dwindle. Ella likens the Deaf child to a tree, then argues that if the hearing mother and the Deaf people don't work together to create a loving, nurturing environment, their struggle over the child is like a saw that will bring down the tree.

The poem is both beautifully constructed and morally persuasive. How does its message influence your thinking about the survival of Deaf culture?

*End of Unit 15*

# Unit 15
## KEY PHRASES

Ask nationality of name (NYE)

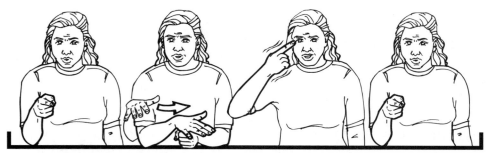

Ask if full-blooded Chinese

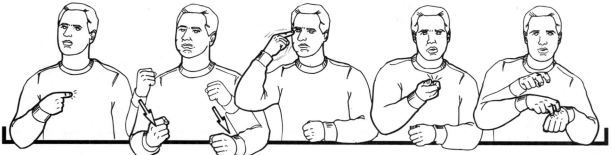

Give nationality (predominantly Chinese, with a bit of Irish)

Tell about unexpected changes (leaving college due to illness)

Tell approximate year you moved to California

Tell when Jose remarried

Tell when you started teaching

Tell how long after you bought the house your son was born

Tell how men moved to Canada to avoid the draft

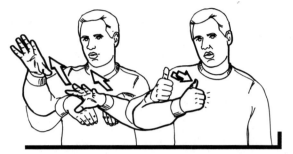

# VOCABULARY REVIEW

JOSE'S LIFE EVENTS

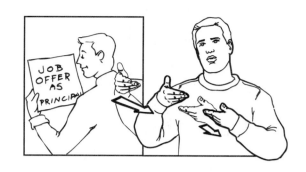

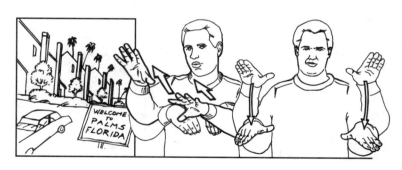

UNEXPECTED CHANGES

TIME SIGNS

*Definition*:
From then until now; during the period between the time given and now; the continuation of an activity/event until now...i.e., for the past number of days, months, years. The sign functions as an adverb. The sign follows the establishment of the activity/event in a sentence.)

*Definition*:
Prior to an event or a specified time.

*Definition*:
Indicate that an unspecified period of time elapsed between events.

DESCRIBING ETHNIC MAKE UP

Japanese

Greek    Finnish

French    Italian

POINTS OF A COMPASS

CONTINENTS

Africa

Africa *

Asia

Australia

Europe

North America

South America

COUNTRIES

Austria

Austria *

Canada

China

Cuba

Denmark

Denmark *

Egypt

* Signs representing countries are shown in the traditional ASL forms. Variations of some of these signs are marked with an asterisk.

England

Finland

Finland *

France

Germany

Greece

Holland

Holland *

Hong Kong

India

Iran

Iraq

Ireland

Israel/Jewish

Italy

Japan

Japan *

Korea

Mexico

Mexico *

Norway

Philippines

Poland

Puerto Rico

Russia

Scotland

Spain

Sweden

Sweden *

Switzerland

Taiwan

Vietnam

Yugoslavia

Yugoslavia*

**INSTITUTIONS:**
    Religion
    Law
    Government

**WHY PEOPLE MOVE:**
    Economic depression

**WHY PEOPLE MOVE:**
    Natural disasters

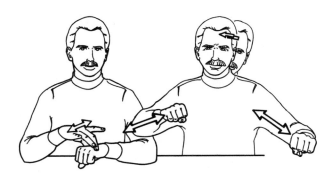 

**WHY PEOPLE MOVE:**
    Persecution

# UNIT 15

WHY PEOPLE MOVE:
   War

WHY PEOPLE MOVE:
Civil disorders

WHY PEOPLE MOVE:
Education

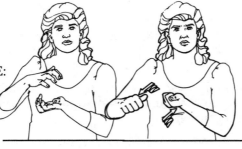 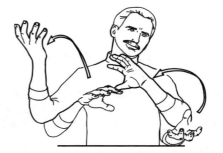

LEAVING
A PLACE

RESPONSES TO FAR-FETCHED
STATEMENTS

86

# UNIT 16
## Describing and Identifying Things

### LANGUAGE IN ACTION

## Have Clock, Will Travel

Read the situation below before watching the videotaped conversation "Have Clock, Will Travel." Then watch the tape and try to follow the intent of the exchange. Let context and the conversation as a whole help you figure out the meaning of unfamiliar signs.

**Situation:** During a football game, Ethan spots Pat who works at the bookstore of a local Deaf services agency. Ethan asks Pat about travel alarm clocks that the bookstore sells.

| | |
|---|---|
| *Ethan:* | gets Pat's attention, greets her, asks if she still works at the DCARA* bookstore |
| *Pat:* | says yes |
| *Ethan:* | asks if DCARA still sells travel clocks |
| *Pat:* | **describes the two models they sell** |
| *Ethan:* | asks how much they cost |
| *Pat:* | gives prices |
| *Ethan:* | asks if he can come by tomorrow to buy one |
| *Pat:* | (starts to respond, but their conversation is interrupted by someone climbing the bleachers) |
| *Ethan:* | asks Pat to repeat |
| *Pat:* | explains they are out of stock, but can order one which would arrive in two weeks |
| *Ethan:* | explains he is leaving in a few days, asks where else he can buy one |
| *Pat:* | tells where he can order one |
| *Ethan:* | asks Pat if they have overnight delivery |
| *Pat:* | says yes, if he uses a credit card |
| *Ethan:* | thanks Pat |

* Acronym for Deaf Counseling, Advocacy and Referral Agency, a Deaf services agency in the San Francisco Bay Area.

Watch the conversation again, focusing on the descriptions Pat gives to compare the two models. Then draw the two clocks based on her descriptions, and write in the prices and other features of each model below.

|  |  |
|---|---|
|  |  |

first model                                    second model

_____                    _____

_____                    _____

_____                    _____

_____                    _____

_____                    _____

Answers on p. 162.

**Getting attention**. Watch the conversation once more and observe how Ethan tries to get Pat's attention. When at first Pat doesn't see Ethan's wave, the man sitting next to Ethan taps the boy sitting near Pat, then Ethan asks the boy to get her attention for him. Once Pat turns to look at Ethan, notice how the boy checks to make sure they have a clear sightline.

**Resuming the conversation**. Notice how Ethan asks Pat to repeat what she said after being interrupted by someone climbing up the bleachers. Observe how Pat resumes the conversation.

# LANGUAGE IN PRACTICE

## Describing Things Around Us

Describing the physical appearance of the things around us is an important part of how we identify things, discriminate between things or define them. Describing an object fluently requires skills in visualizing the object, choosing appropriate classifiers, and using the interplay of the weak and dominant hands.

## Using Classifiers to Describe Things

**1) Descriptive classifiers (DCLs)**: These classifier handshapes categorize nouns by their physical characteristics. To describe an object, select a classifier handshape to describe its basic shape and size, i.e., sphere, cube, cylinder. See the illustrations of basic shapes with their corresponding DCLs.

Use non-manual behaviors, particularly the mouth, to emphasize the size of theobject if it is unusual, or if you are contrasting two similar objects of different sizes. For example:

| | | |
|---|---|---|
| mouth "oo": relatively small | mouth "mm": standard size | mouth "cha": relatively large |

Notice also how the handshape of the DCL varies according to the size of the object.

DCLs are also used to describe *attachments and designs* on objects. How you describe attachments and designs depends on whether they are symmetrical or asymmetrical in relation to the basic shape of the object.

If the attachments are *symmetrical* (the attachments on both sides are similar in size and shape), describe the object by first establishing its basic shape, then using both hands simultaneously to show the attachments in their relative locations. See the illustration below of a signer describing a rolling pin.

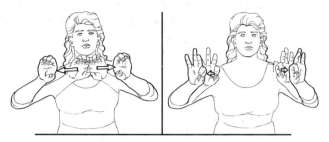

If the attachments are *asymmetrical* (with different attachments on both sides, or an attachment on one side only), establish the basic shape with both hands, then use your weak hand to hold the reference point while your dominant hand shows the attachments in their relative locations. See the illustration below of a signer describing a pitcher.

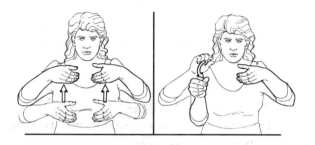

**2) Instrument classifiers (ICLs):** Another way to describe attachments is to describe how the object is handled or how it works. Instrument classifiers are classifier handshapes and movements that indicate how an object or an attachment is handled, i.e., how it is pushed, pulled, lifted, turned. Here are some examples of how to use ICLs as part of a description: to indicate a pull-cord on a lamp, show how it is pulled; to indicate an oven door, show how you open it with the handle; to indicate a light switch on the wall, show how it is switched on and off.

## The Science Lab

In the next videotaped segment, Freda demonstrates descriptions of all of the objects pictured on the following page in the context of a skit. She plays the role of a scatterbrained scientist who asks Ben, her slow-witted assistant, to get various objects to set up an experiment.

Observe how Freda contrasts sizes and distinctive features to clarify which object she means. Also observe how she uses her weak hand as a reference point.

**Using reference points.** Afterwards, you will see clips from the skit in slow motion. The clips show you how the scientist uses her weak hand (her left hand) to retain the DCL handshape for the basic shape while describing the additional features with her dominant hand (her right hand). Practice by imitating these descriptions.

## PRACTICE

Practice describing the objects illustrated below using descriptive and instrument classifiers. Remember to use your weak hand as a reference point whenever you describe asymmetrical attachments, either by how they look or how they are handled. Remember also to "look at" the object you describe as if you are really seeing it.

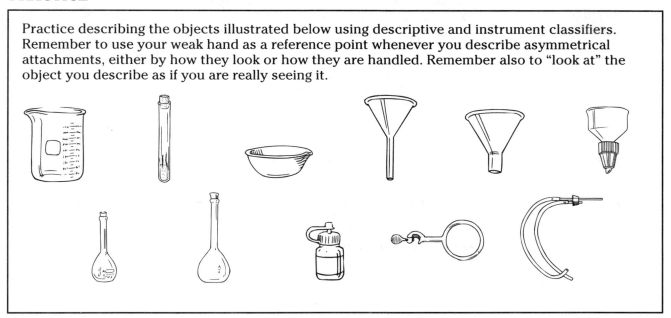

## General Sequences for Describing Objects

**Describing objects that are not fixed.** By "not fixed" we mean things that are portable and unattached to any surface, such as accessories, small appliances, food items. The objects in the Science Lab demonstration are examples of things that are not fixed.

The amount and kind of information you give in describing an object depends on the purpose of your description. It also depends on how familiar your listener is with the object you describe. Your purpose and/or emphasis will affect the sequence you use, but in general, follow this sequence to describe how something looks:

- Give the name of the object and/or tell what material it's made of (i.e., wood, metal, glass, plastic).
- Tell the color of the object or its parts, if relevant.
- Use a DCL to establish the basic shape and size of the object. Use non-manual behaviors to emphasize an unusual size or to contrast similar objects of different sizes.
- Using the basic shape as a reference point, use other DCLs to describe distinctive features, attachments, or designs.
- Use ICLs to indicate how the object or its attachments are handled or used, if relevant.

**Describing fixed objects**. Some objects have a "fixed" position, i.e., they may be attached to the ceiling or placed in a certain position on the floor and not normally moved around. For example, a floor lamp, bed, light fixture, refrigerator, and fire hydrant are considered fixed. The basic sequence for describing how something looks is the same (i.e., tell what it is or what it's made of, tell the color if relevant, then describe the object). However, there are other conventions to follow for describing fixed objects. The sequence of your description depends on which of the following categories the object fits into:

- **Describe from bottom to top:** If the object is columnar and standing upright on the floor or ground, describe the basic shape from bottom to top, then add details. For example, to describe a floor lamp, begin by describing its base, then the pole, then describe the shape of its shade or top, and finally identify what kind of switch or pull-cord it has. Other objects in this category are a telephone pole, tree, stool, fire hydrant, street lamp.

- **Describe from top to bottom:** If the object is bulky and standing on the floor or ground, first describe the basic shape from top to bottom, then add details. For example, to describe a refrigerator, indicate the basic shape (with both hands in the B-handshape) starting with the top, then the sides. Then describe the type of door(s) it has with ICLs. Other objects in this category are a console TV, dresser, stove, table, boulder.

- **Describe from the ceiling down:** If the object is columnar and hanging from the ceiling, describe the object from the ceiling down, then add details. For example, to describe a hanging lamp, begin with the chain or cable that attaches the lamp to the ceiling, then describe the shape of the light fixture, and end with the pull-cord or switch. Other objects in this category are a hanging plant, mobile, icicles, stalactites in a cave.

Some objects that are, in fact, fixed or not portable are still described in neutral space. Objects that have an unusual shape, or that are too large to describe in their actual dimensions, are abstracted into a smaller size. For example, the basic shape of a sofa, rocking chair or sports car might all be described in neutral space, following the sequence for objects that are not fixed, and described from different perspectives to furnish details.

## Determining Perspectives

One final consideration in describing objects is determining the proper perspective to describe it from. Below are the perspectives used for different kinds of objects:

- **Describe from the front:** If the object has a definite front and back, describe it as if you were standing in front of it. Objects in this category are a TV, typewriter, computer, radio, blender, dresser, VCR, sofa, headboard, TTY.

- **Describe in neutral space:** If the object has no definite front or back, describe it in neutral space. Objects in this category are a dining table, coffee table, toaster, pots and pans, basket, plant, lamp.

- **Describe from the rear:** If the object is usually handled from the rear, describe it as if you were using it, i.e., camcorder held on your shoulder, binoculars held up to your eyes. Other objects in this category are a camera, telescope, kaleidoscope, megaphone.

- **Describe from a sitting position:** If the object is usually seen from a sitting position, describe attachments (i.e., foot rest of a recliner, arm rests, turn signals on a steering wheel) as seen in that position. Objects in this category are a sofa, chair, car, bicycle.

- **Describe as if on your body:** If the object is used on a person's body, describe it as if you were wearing it. Objects in this category are clothing, eyeglasses, cap, gloves, uniform, mask.

Certain objects can also be described as seen from inside (for example, the description of the tent in the next videotaped activity). This is similar to describing a room from the perspective of the doorway, as you learned in Unit 13.

# Describing Objects

On videotape, you will see signers describing various objects. Watch how Mary describes the vase and Guy describes the football helmet using the following sequence:

1.         identify object:     vase
             identify color:     white
             identify size:     a little over a foot tall
    describe basic shape:     cylinder
      describe details:     spiral design
      perspective used:     no front
      type of sequence:     not fixed

2.         identify object:     L.A. Rams football helmet
    describe basic shape:     spherical
      describe details:     face mask, logo on side, chin strap
      perspective used:     on body
      type of sequence:     not fixed

Now fill in the blanks below according to the descriptions signed on tape.

3.     identify object: *Lamp*
    identify material: *metal and glass*
    describe basic shape: *Curved with Rod going thru it.*
    describe details: *Shade wide band At base folded Design, pull chain*
    perspective used: *Ceiling Lamp*
    type of sequence: *Started At top Described materials, Did Not Describe Base.*

4.     identify object: *Free standing old gas Range*
    identify material: *metal*
    describe basic shape: *Tall, Shaped Like A Refrigerator*
    describe details: *many compartments, food warmer on top, main oven, Side Broiler, controls on Right*
    perspective used: *cooking*
    type of sequence: *Described Size, oven, Broiler, Controls etc.*

93

CL= classifiers

**5.** identify object: Sofa w/ 1/4 having Leg Rest
describe basic shape: Wing back, Leg rest comes up
identify color/pattern: Blue and White
describe details: Leg Rest control on Right, Soft, Descri'bd Actions of Leg Rest
perspective used: Relaxing, Watching T.V
type of sequence: chair, Soft Color, Leg rest

**6.** identify object: Cam corder
describe basic shape: Boxish Rests on Shoulder
identify size: Shoe Box Size
describe details: Uses Reg VCR tape, Zoom, Light can view tape, auto controls Rewind Runs hour. Built in eye piece
perspective used: Home movies
type of sequence: Size, Location, function,

**7.** identify object: Dome pop-up tent
describe basic shape: Dome shape
describe details: Metal poles, Zipper Door, windows, Flaps Sleeps 3 poles connect together, Fabric connects to poles, has floor
perspective used: Camping
type of sequence: Shape, Construction, how Assembled, how many sleeps, features

Answers on p. 162.

Watch the descriptions again to see the <u>instrument classifiers</u> used to show how parts of the objects are handled:

- ceiling lamp: Lon uses an ICL to represent the pull-cord
- stove: Cinnie uses ICLs to represent turning the knobs on the stove and pulling the handles on the oven and compartment doors
- couch: Lon uses an ICL to represent pulling the lever on the recliner
- camcorder: Mary uses ICLs to represent pushing various buttons on the camcorder and inserting the videotape
- tent: Cinnie uses ICLs to represent zipping up the door and window

The following descriptions include several examples of using the weak hand as a reference point while describing attachments:

- Mary's description of the vase
- Lon's description of the ceiling lamp
- Cinnie's description of the stove
- Mary's description of the camcorder (In this example, her dominant hand establishes the reference point because of the way the camcorder is actually held.)

# Picture It

Several signers will each describe an object. Visualize the object as they describe it. After each description, stop the tape and draw the object as accurately as possible.

Answers on p. 163.

# Potpourri

On videotape, you will see six minidialogues in which one signer identifies an object. Notice that the amount and kind of description depend on why the signer is describing the object, and on the other person's familiarity with it.*

### Minidialogue 1

| | |
|---|---|
| *Tina Jo*: | asks what lopping shears are |
| *Mary*: | tells what they are used for |
| *Tina Jo*: | describes object to confirm |
| *Mary*: | corrects, tells how the two shears are different |
| *Tina Jo*: | responds (somewhat familiar) |

Circle the illustration below that matches the description of lopping shears. Then cross out the illustration that matches the description of the other shears.

### Minidialogue 2

| | |
|---|---|
| *Ramona*: | describes object, asks if familiar |
| *Dan*: | responds affirmatively (very familiar) |
| *Ramona*: | asks what it's called |
| *Dan*: | spells out name of object |
| *Ramona*: | responds |

Name the object Ramona describes: ___EDGER___

### Minidialogue 3

| | |
|---|---|
| *Cinnie*: | explains what her husband gave her for her birthday |
| *Ethan*: | asks for more description |
| *Cinnie*: | gives additional details |
| *Ethan*: | responds (quite familiar), gives opinion |
| *Cinnie*: | responds |

Circle the illustration below that matches the description of the camera Cinnie received from her husband.

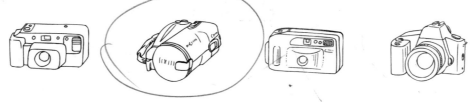

---

* When describing an object to identify it, describe as much as necessary until the other person acknowledges s/he knows what you mean. Sometimes the listener will recognize the object you mean after one or two details; other times further description is needed.

**Minidialogue 4**

*Ivanetta*:    identifies food dish (chicken fajitas)

*Priscilla*:    responds (very familiar)

*Ivanetta*:    asks how to make it

*Priscilla*:    explains process of making it

*Ivanetta*:    responds

Name the ingredients Priscilla uses to make chicken fajitas:

Cut up chicken, Red pepper yellow pepper cook in Butter, warm up tortias and Roll up & Eat.

**Minidialogue 5**

*Steve*:    identifies plant in bedroom

*Shane*:    gives additional details to confirm

*Steve*:    corrects by telling its location

*Shane*:    responds, gives additional details to confirm

*Steve*:    confirms, asks favor

*Shane*:    agrees

*Steve*:    responds

How are the two plants different from each other?

One has flowers, other is tall needs water

**Minidialogue 6**

*Lon*:    asks what needlepoint is

*Carlene*:    gives definition by how it looks

*Lon*:    asks if it is similar to rug hooking

*Carlene*:    corrects, contrasts needlepoint with rug hooking

*Lon*:    responds

What are two differences between needlepoint and rug hooking?

One uses fine thread and long knots the other uses thick & short thread, knots and is tough Different stitch, hooks.

Answers on p. 163.

Now go back and watch the dialogues again and try to imitate the descriptions.

## What's a Sashimi?

Watch the dialogue on videotape and observe how Ivanetta describes various dishes to Anthony, who is not familiar with Japanese food.

| | |
|---|---|
| *Anthony:* | asks what sashimi is |
| *Ivanetta:* | **gives definition by telling how it is made** |
| *Anthony:* | asks if it's similar to sushi |
| *Ivanetta:* | responds, **compares** sashimi and sushi |
| *Anthony:* | responds, asks what sukiyaki is |
| *Ivanetta:* | **describes it** |
| *Anthony:* | responds by saying he doesn't care for that kind of food |
| *Ivanetta:* | suggests tempura |
| *Anthony:* | responds, asks what it is |
| *Ivanetta:* | **describes by telling how it is made,** gives opinion |
| *Anthony:* | asks if it's spicy hot |
| *Ivanetta:* | says no, contrasts Japanese and Chinese food |
| *Anthony:* | accepts her suggestion |

(waitress returns to take their orders, then leaves)

*Anthony:* ⎫
*Ivanetta:* ⎬ discuss the appropriateness of certain gestures

Write your answers to the following questions:

**1.** Describe the difference between sashimi and sushi.

  GNC IS Served oN Rica the other the Rice is
  ON the side

**2.** Ivanetta says sukiyaki is similar to ___Soup___.

**3.** Tempura is ___Shrimp___ and ___veg.___ dipped in ___flour___, then deep fried in ___oil___.

Answers on p. 163.

## Money Number Signs

On videotape, you will see Cinnie, Lon, and Sandra demonstrate the following number signs for amounts between $1.01 and $9.99. Watch closely at the orientation and movement of each number: for dollar amounts less than $10, the dollar number is twisted towards the signer's body, followed by the number for cents signed with the palm facing outward.

| | | | | | |
|---|---|---|---|---|---|
| $1.01 | $6.06 | $2.10 | $7.60 | $1.81 | $6.36 |
| $2.02 | $7.07 | $3.20 | $8.70 | $2.72 | $7.27 |
| $3.03 | $8.08 | $4.30 | $9.80 | $3.63 | $8.18 |
| $4.04 | $9.09 | $5.40 | $1.90 | $4.54 | $9.99 |
| $5.05 | | $6.50 | | $5.45 | |

Practice signing the numbers demonstrated on tape.

# Matching Costs with Objects

On videotape, you will see different signers describe an object, then tell how much it costs. Look at the pictures below to find the appropriate object, then write down the cost in the blank. (Not all objects pictured will be described.)

34⁰⁰   6 ⁸⁹.   25 ⁰⁰   67⁰⁰   95⁰⁰   14 ⁹⁵

42⁰⁰   379   7 ⁵⁰   60 ⁰⁰   18 ⁰⁰   3 ²⁵

4 ⁹⁵.   25 ⁰⁰   _____   75 ⁰⁰   70 ⁰⁰   8 ⁹.

_____   5 ³³   45 ⁰⁰   55 ⁰⁰   _____   8 ⁹⁹

Answers on p. 163.

# History of TTYs

Pat traces the history and evolution of teletypewriters (TTYs) from the early 1960s to the present.*
Even though the new, smaller electronic devices may be called Telecommunication Devices for the
Deaf (TDDs), Deaf people still often prefer the term TTY. After watching this segment of the tape,
answer the questions below.

**1.** How did Deaf people get in touch with each other a long time ago?

**2.** Fill in developments that occurred over the years:

1960s _Western Union Discards old_
_teletypwriter, picked up converted._

1970 _Smaller portable No printer_
_Weisbright, George Involved in Development._

1975 _printers ADDED 7" wide Later_
_paper size increase, Ink to thermal._

1981 _Calif. &rue TDD. Soon Spreads to_
_other States, government support_

1990 _Smaller pocket Size Battery_
_powered, Direct connect, Avail on payphone._

_TTY - Deaf NAme_
_TTD - Hearing_
_TT Phone company_

**3.** What were the disadvantages of the original teletypewriters?
_Large heavy Bulky, Elect often Broke Down_

**4.** With these old machines, how did Pat know it was her turn to talk?
_Stopped Shaking, stopped printing_

**5.** What is appealing about the latest device to come on the market?
_Lightweight easy to use memory, Battery power_
_Pocket Size, cellular. Avail for computer use,_
_Answering machine._

Answers on p. 164.

---

* TTYs are telecommunication devices that enable deaf people to use the telephone. The deaf person places the receiver on
a coupler attached to the TTY. The device has a small keyboard and the conversation takes place by typing back and forth.

# The Story Corner

**"Reveille"**

At the beginning of his narrative, Ethan explains how Deaf people have it easy nowadays with special alarm clocks that are attached to either a flashing light or a bed vibrator. He then goes on to describe some of the ways Deaf people used to wake themselves up when electric alarm clocks were not available. The information is taken from Byron B. Burnes's article "Reveille." Be sure to ask your instructor for a copy of the article (pp. 148–149 of the *Teacher's Curriculum Guide*). Written descriptions of the various devices are provided below. After you have watched the narrative, practice describing the devices yourself.

- Dormitory supervisor wakes up students by shaking every bed.

- A string and pulley arrangement suspends a flatiron near the ceiling. The alarm clock trips a release, dropping the iron to the floor.

- A person tightly clutches an old-fashioned alarm clock through the night.

- A string is tied onto one person's wrist, while the person in the next bed holds the other end. When the alarm goes off under the second person's pillow, s/he jerks the string and wakes the first person up.

- Two slats are hinged together, then attached to the head of the bed. One slat hangs from the hinge, while the other has a hook which is attached to the key on the back of an alarm clock. When the alarm sounds, the unwinding key pulls on the hook, and the top slat slams down against its counterpart with a bang.

- A box-like arrangement, long and narrow, stands vertically at the head of the bed. Within the box are a number of small shelves, one above the other, sloping gently downward, and on the top shelf rests a small version of a cannon ball. The ball is held in place on the top shelf by a connection with the alarm key. When the alarm sounds, the key releases the ball, which rolls off the shelf, hits the next one, rolls on to the next, and so on until it shakes the sleeper awake.

- A different slat contrivance is attached to the foot of the bed, and instead of banging against another slat to produce a loud retort, it slams down right upon the sleeper.

# LANGUAGE IN PERFORMANCE

## Storytelling

Storytelling holds a place of special importance in cultures whose language has no written form. Deaf children learn the art of storytelling at residential schools for the Deaf—they learn how to vividly re-create events and characters from Deaf adults who use ASL fluently. Members of the Deaf community commonly agree that storytelling is the most popular form of signed entertainment. The storyteller, the story, and the audience all play an important role in the success of the telling. The storyteller, skilled with language, draws the audience in; the story, full of life, holds the attention of the audience; finally the audience gives its approval by repeating the story to others.

### "The Ball" by Ben Bahan

Sam Supalla introduces Ben Bahan's story, "The Ball," a unique ASL story in which Ben artfully uses semantic classifiers to represent various characters chasing after a runaway ball. These classifiers represent certain nouns such as vehicles, persons, four-legged animals, etc., and are used to show movement. The classifiers Ben uses in this story are listed below, with the nouns they represent in parentheses:

| | |
|---|---|
| 3-handshape | (bicycle with a boy on it) |
| bent-V-handshape | (dog) |
| 1-handshape | (girl on rollerskates) |
| bent-1-handshape | (old man) |
| horizontal-1-handshape | (flying bird) |
| Y-handshape | (fat woman) |

He shows each character following the others as they chase the ball in different directions, around corners, uphill and down. He modifies the signs and his non-manual behaviors to reflect the manner and qualities of each character. As Sam mentions in his introduction, the story is like many classic children's stories, using repetition to create a special cadence. This repetition follows a series of events that builds to a dramatic climax.

*End of Unit 16*

102

# Unit 16
## KEY PHRASES

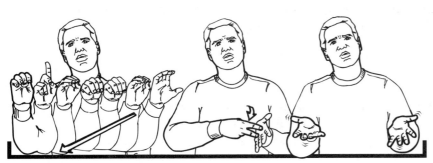

Ask what is a commode

Tell what a commode is by describing it

Ask how much it costs

Tell how much it costs (75 dollars)

Ask what is a tostada

Tell what is a tostada by describing how it is made

Describe the tool (ratchet) and ask what it is called

# VOCABULARY REVIEW

DESCRIBE PATTERNS ON
OBJECTS AND SURFACES

Lines

poka Dots

grate

mixed Designs

coiled wavy

Thin Line
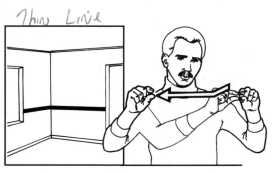

Long thin
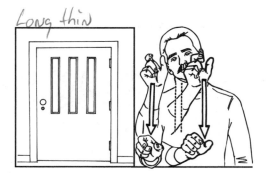

DESCRIBE SURFACES

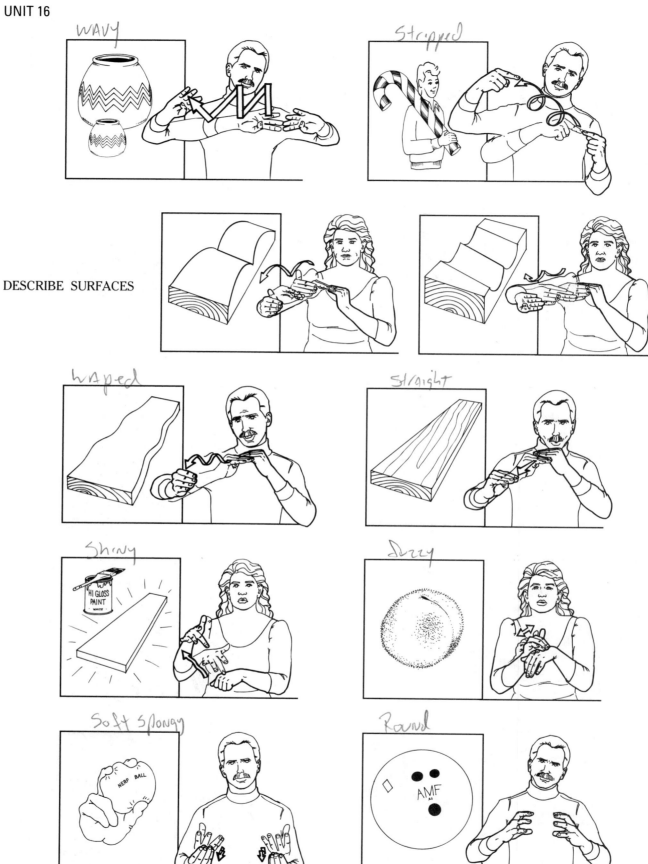

WHAT THINGS ARE MADE OF

wood

Metal

plastic

Rubber

glass

Cloth

PAper

CHARGE IT

NEWS
BUDGET
APPROVED

WAYS TO PREPARE FOOD

cook

Boil under flame

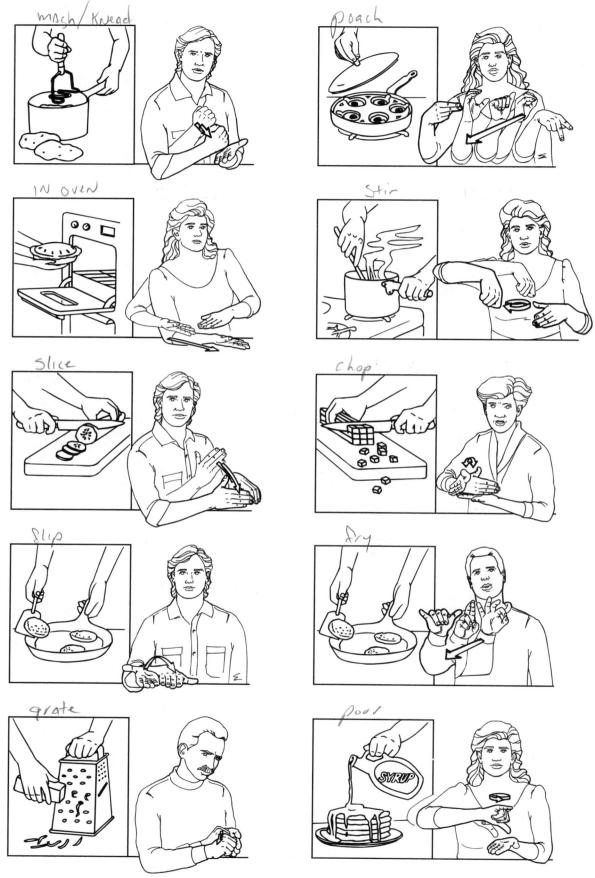

mash/knead

poach

IN oven

stir

slice

chop

flip

fry

grate

pour

SYRUP

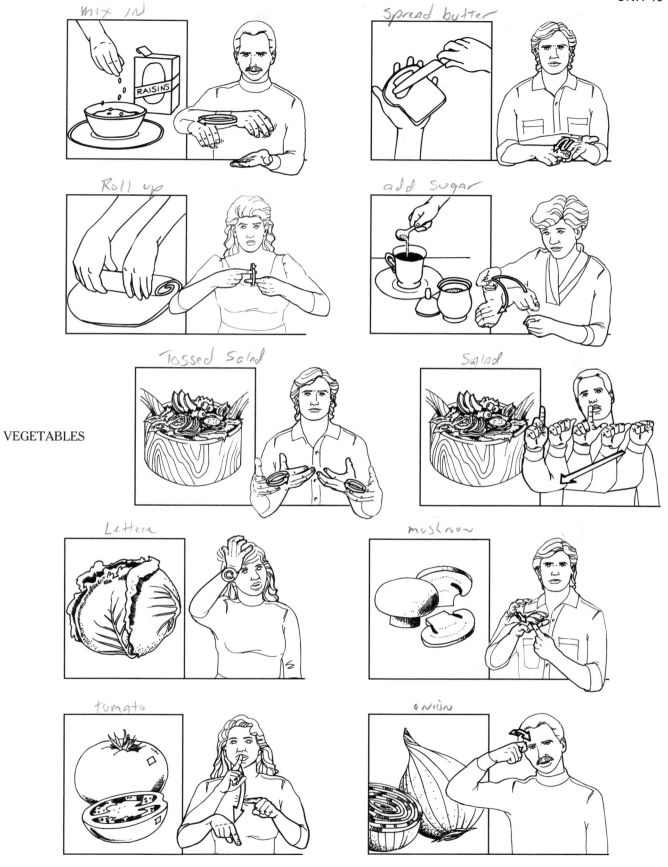

mix in

spread butter

Roll up

add sugar

Tossed Salad

Salad

VEGETABLES

Lettuce

mushroom

tomato

onion

carrot
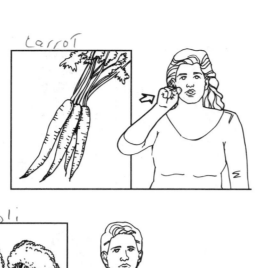

corn
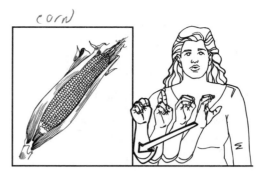

broccoli

cauliflower

Green pepper

tofu

String beans

potato

MEATS

Beef

meat
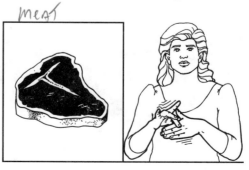

pork

ham

bacon

fish

chicken

turkey

hamburger

hot dog

DAIRY PRODUCTS

cheese

sour cream

butter

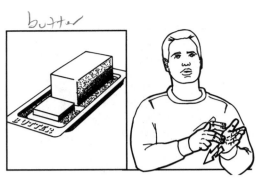

eggs

milk

ice cream

yogurt

CONDIMENTS

jam

sugar

mustard

mAyo

Ketchup

Salt pepper

Relish

cherry

FRUITS

grapes

ORANge

BANANA

pineapple

113

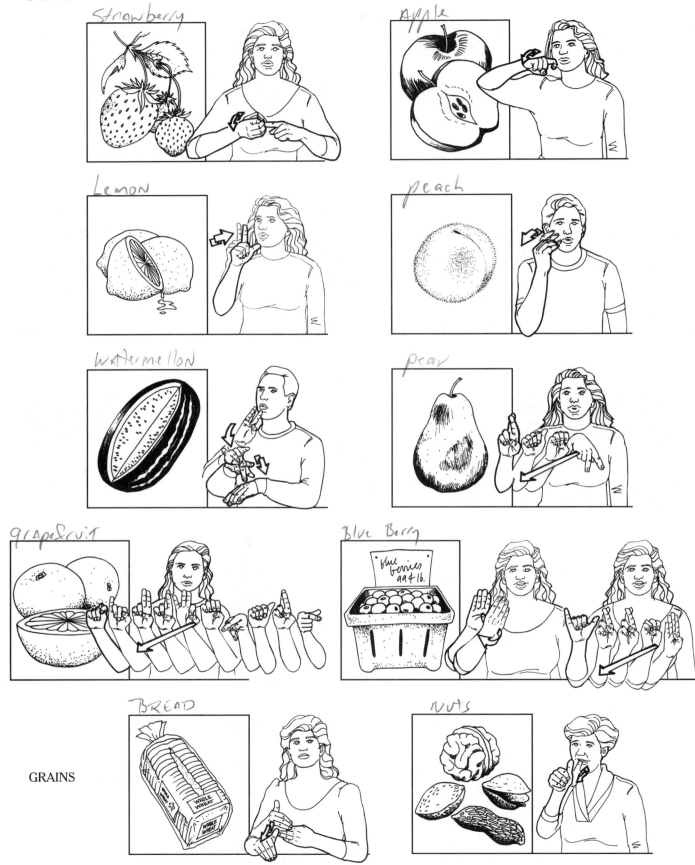

Strawberry

Apple

Lemon

peach

watermellon

pear

grapefruit

Blue Berry

GRAINS

BREAD

nuts

114

RICE

OPINIONS OF FOOD

delicious          horrible

HOW FOOD TASTES

sweet

sour

spicy-hot

greasy

MONEY NUMBERS

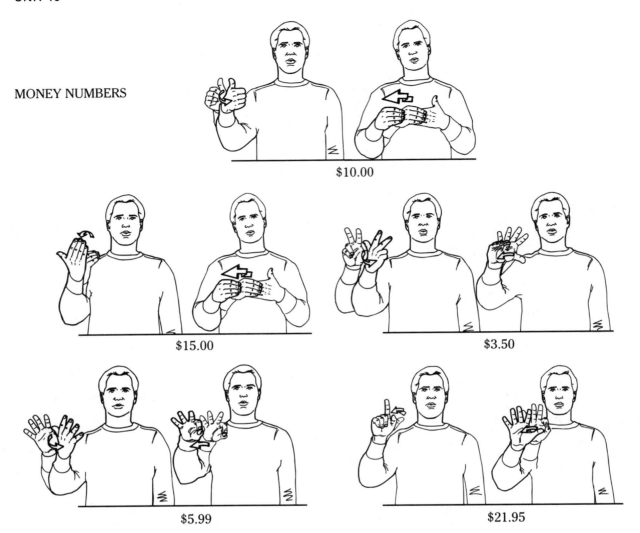

$10.00

$15.00

$3.50

$5.99

$21.95

# UNIT 17

*(Devolus Test)*

# * Talking About the Weekend *

## LANGUAGE IN ACTION

## Places to See in Seattle

Read the situation below before watching the videotaped conversation "Places to See in Seattle." Then watch the tape and try to follow the intent of the exchange. Let context and the conversation as a whole help you figure out the meaning of unfamiliar signs.

**Situation:** Anthony asks Lon to suggest several things to see and do in Seattle.

| | |
|---|---|
| *Anthony:* | asks if Lon has ever been to Seattle, Washington |
| *Lon:* | replies affirmatively, says he's been there several times, gives opinion |
| *Anthony:* | tells Lon he will go there in two weeks |
| *Lon:* | asks if it is Anthony's first time there |
| *Anthony:* | replies affirmatively, asks Lon for ideas on places to see or things to do in Seattle |
| *Lon:* | recommends three things to see or do: the Space Needle, Pike's Market, and ferries to the islands, Olympic National Park or Victoria |
| *Anthony:* | asks Lon to elaborate on each place |
| *Lon:* | gives more information |
| *Anthony:* | responds |

**Controlling the pace of conversation**. Watch the conversation again, focusing on how the signers regulate the flow of conversation by slowing, holding, or repeating signs while Lon ties his shoes.

**Plural classifiers**. Also notice how Lon uses three different plural classifiers (see Unit 13, p. 15): for hordes of people going to Pike's Market, many flowers in Victoria, many unusual things sold at Pike's Market.

Summarize the information Lon gives about each place, and write Lon's opinion below.

1. Space Needle: _See the city, Rest. AT top, Rotates_
   _expensive good food_

   Opinion: _Very Nice worth seeing_

2. Pike's Market: _Lots of Different Shops, imports old furnation_
   _hard to find things_

   Opinion: _To Crowded_

3. Ferry to Victoria: _Six hour trip very Nice costs About $25.00_
   _Sit inside or outside Nice gardens and views_

   Opinion: _Nice trip worth trying._

Answers on p. 164.

117

# LANGUAGE IN PRACTICE

## Narrating About Weekend Activities

In this unit, the narratives telling about weekend activities have an introduction, a main body that includes a series of activities in chronological order, and a closing that is often an opinion or evaluation of the weekend. To make a narrative coherent, signers should use clear transitions and maintain continuity.

**Transitions.** Throughout the body of these narratives, signers make transitions from one part of the day to the next by using time signs, for example, signs for "last night" or "Saturday morning." Within each part of the day any number of activities or events could be discussed, but the end of one part and the beginning of the next must be "marked" to make it easy for the listener to follow. The following non-manual behaviors accompany the transitional time signs: a slight pause and head nod that marks the end of one part, and raised eyebrows with the time sign to mark the beginning of the next part. You will see many examples of these non-manual behaviors in the narratives.

**Continuity.** All the time in an entire signed narrative tends to be accounted for, which creates a sense of continuity. A common way of accounting for time is using *durative time signs*, which indicate how long an activity continued (see the illustrations below for some examples). Durative time signs usually occur at the *end* of the description of activities during that part of the day.

Another way to maintain continuity is to use *continuous inflection* on certain verbs, by repeating the verb sign with a circular movement. This shows that an activity went on for a period of time.* For example:

* See Unit 14, p. 37, to review verbs with continuous inflection.

118

A third way to show continuity is to account for movement between places. Often this is done with certain signs that show a natural *beginning and end*, or coming and going. See the illustrations of possible "beginning-end pairs" below.

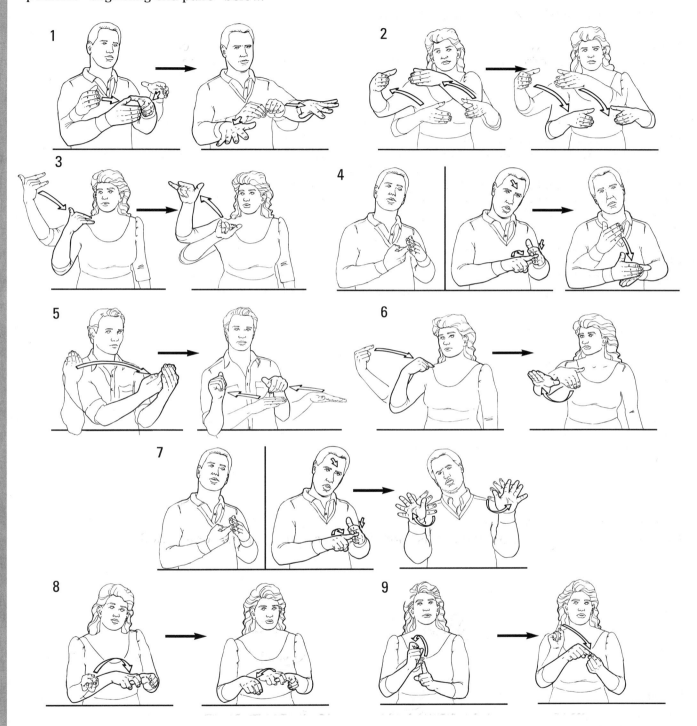

You may substitute similar signs for either of the paired signs in the illustrations. Also, the second sign of the pair does not have to immediately follow the first; other signs may be included between them. The important thing is to include enough information. Don't leave your listener stranded: if you say you went by bus to one place, you should also say that you got back from there. If you don't account for time or movement, your listener may feel something is missing from your narrative.

## Trip for Two

Watch the next videotaped narrative in which Lon tells about his trip to Colorado. We have identified the **transitions** throughout the main body of the narrative: each part begins at the time code listed below.

*Introduction:* Lon explains that he won a free trip for two to Colorado.

*Main Body:*

transitions

| | | | |
|---|---|---|---|
| (00:14) | On Friday... | (01:33) | That night... |
| (00:32) | That night... | (01:51–52) | At 9:30... |
| (00:53–54) | The next morning... | (01:56) | In the morning... |
| (01:06) | At noon... | (02:10–11) | In the early afternoon... |
| (01:16–17) | At five... | | |

*Closing:* Lon gives his opinion of the weekend.

Now watch the tape again to see how Lon **maintains continuity** throughout the narrative. Examples of maintaining continuity occur within the time codes listed below.

| | |
|---|---|
| (00:23) – (00:25) beginning-end pair | (01:23) – (01:26) beginning-end pair |
| (00:44) – (00:45) durative time sign | (01:43) – (01:45) verbs with continuous inflection |
| (00:51) – (00:53) durative time sign | (01:54) – (01:56) durative time sign |
| (00:56) – (00:59) beginning-end pair | (02:08) – (02:10) durative time sign |
| (01:04) – (01:06) durative time sign | (02:15) – (02:18) beginning-end pair |
| (01:14) – (01:15) durative time sign | (02:19) – (02:21) beginning-end pair |

## The Signing Weekend

Now watch the next videotaped narrative in which Mary tells Cinnie about her experience at a Signing Weekend. This time identify the **transitions** yourself: write down the time code at the beginning of each part of the narrative (see the example in "Trip for Two" above).

*Introduction:* Cinnie introduces the topic herself by asking Mary about the Silent Weekend.

*Main Body:*

transitions

1. _____       5. _____

2. _____       6. _____

3. _____       7. _____

4. _____       8. _____

*Closing:* Mary gives her opinion of the weekend.

Notice how Mary **maintains continuity** by showing how groups of people moved from place to place. Look at the parts between time codes (00:50) – (01:07) and (01:08) – (01:28) for examples.

Answers on p. 164.

# Beginning Conversations

Narratives usually occur within conversations, unless they're told as stories on stage. In the dialogues on videotape, the descriptions of weekend activities are introduced in various ways. Watch the dialogues, focusing on how the subject is brought up. Then fill in the information requested below.

**Dialogue 1:** Anthony explains to Ethan, his boss, why he couldn't finish his assignment over the weekend.

**1.** Summarize what happened over the weekend.
Friday:

Saturday:

Sunday:

**2.** How was the topic of the weekend brought up?

**Dialogue 2:** Yolanda asks Sandra about her garden project.

**1.** Summarize what happened over the weekend.
Friday:

Saturday:

Sunday:

**2.** How was the topic of the weekend brought up?

**Dialogue 3:** Ethan's weekend plans were cancelled. He tells Joe, his co-worker, what happened.

**1.** Summarize what happened over the weekend.
Friday:

Saturday:

**2.** How was the topic of the weekend brought up?

**Dialogue 4:** Mary runs into Tina Jo at the gym, and tells her about her weekend.

**1.** Summarize what happened over the weekend.
Friday:

Saturday:

Sunday:

**2.** How was the topic of the weekend brought up?

**Dialogue 5:** Anthony and Yolanda happen to meet on campus. She explains why she didn't go to the party on Saturday night.

**1.** Summarize what happened on Saturday.

**2.** How was the topic brought up?

Answers on pp. 164–165.

Now go back and watch the dialogues again, this time noticing how the signers use time signs to mark transitions and how they maintain continuity throughout their narratives. Dialogue 4, in particular, has a number of good examples.

## Disrupted Plans

Next on the videotape you will see five narratives about how people's weekend plans were disrupted, or how various things went wrong. Notice how the narrators use this sign for telling about a sudden or unexpected change. After each narrative, write your answers to the questions below.

**Narrative 1:** Mary tells how a boat trip didn't work out as planned.

**1.** What was the water like when they left the harbor? What was it like in the open sea?
*Rain Rough Seas*

**2.** What happened after Mary looked out the window?
*Sea Sick*

**3.** What did the captain decide to do?
*Return to Dock*

**4.** What did Mary and the others get when they returned to shore?
*go to hosp.*

**5.** How did Mary feel about the change in plans?

**6.** What word does Mary fingerspell, once with one hand, then again with both hands?

**Narrative 2:** Cinnie describes several mishaps at a wedding.

1. Describe the setting of the wedding.

2. What was the first unexpected occurrence?

3. What was the next unexpected occurrence related to the car?

4. How was the problem solved?

5. What was the last unexpected occurrence?

6. How did people feel about the day?

7. What words does Cinnie fingerspell?

**Narrative 3:** Sandra tells about one weekend in which several things went wrong.

1. What did Sandra and her husband decide to do?

2. What was the first step of the plan?

3. Why was the delay a problem for Sandra?

4. How was the problem solved?

5. Why did they cover all the wood?

6. What happened that night?

7. What was the next disruption?

8. What happened afterwards?

9. What words does Sandra fingerspell?

**Narrative 4:** Lon tells about a series of setbacks on a trip out of town.

**1.** What did Lon think the warning light was at first?

**2.** What was the problem really?

**3.** How did Lon solve the problem?

**4.** Why did Lon run out of gas?

**5.** How did he get gas?

**6.** When did Lon finally arrive at his destination?

**7.** What words does Lon fingerspell?

**Narrative 5:** Malcolm describes a weekend when he went camping.

**1.** What was the first problem Malcolm and his friend encountered?

**2.** How did they solve it?

**3.** What problem occurred the next day?

**4.** What did they decide to do?

**5.** Why did they dunk themselves in the water?

**6.** Did the weather the next day turn out the way they hoped?

**7.** What did they do the next day?

**8.** What words does Malcolm fingerspell?

Answers on pp. 165–166.

# Three-Digit Numbers

Tina Jo, Malcolm and Ivanetta will model three-digit numbers. In the first set, Tina Jo models these numbers:

160   270   310   490   540   680   730   820   950

In the second set, Malcolm models these numbers:

111   222   333   444   555   666   777   888   999

In the third set, Ivanetta models these numbers in which the final two digits are the rocking number forms:

467   868   269   178   379   689   598   797   198   387   986   276

Watch the demonstrations, then practice these number signs.

# Number Practice

On screen, several people will sign sentences incorporating one or two number signs. After watching each sentence, write down the number (or numbers) and the topic to which the number(s) refer.

number(s)                                        topic

1. _____        _____

2. _____        _____

3. _____        _____

4. _____  _____   _____

5. _____  _____   _____

6. _____  _____   _____

7. _____  _____   _____

8. _____  _____   _____

Answers on p. 166.

## Descriptionary: A Game Show

In each round of the Descriptionary game, the English word for an object will appear on screen just before Freda, the host, signs her description of the object. The contestants on the show must guess what the object is by fingerspelling the word.

You are to identify which contestant fingerspelled the correct word by circling the picture of that contestant below.

**Round 1:** spur

**Round 2:** cactus

**Round 3:** sundial

**Round 4:** starfish

**Round 5:** bucket

**Round 6:** sieve

**Round 7:** telescope

**Round 8:** baster

Answers on p. 166.

Now watch the game show again. This time, identify the contestant who spelled each of the words or phrases below. Write the number of the contestant next to the word or phrase s/he spelled.

**Round 1:**

pinwheel _____
wheelbarrow _____
brace _____
edger _____
spur _____

**Round 2:**

coffee rack _____
driftwood _____
hat rack _____
pipes _____
deadwood _____
branches _____
carafe _____
cactus _____

**Round 3:**

wedge _____
ice cream maker _____
butcher block _____
birdbath _____
cardholder _____
cake _____
sundial _____

**Round 4:**

star _____
star of David _____
star jasmine _____
Ninja star _____
snowflake _____
jack _____
jelly fish _____
star of Bethlehem _____
starfish _____

**Round 5:**

basket _____
pail _____
purse _____
bag _____
handbag _____
hip hugger _____
bucket _____

**Round 6:**

strainer _____
basket _____
sieve _____
sifter _____
net _____
deep fryer basket _____
colander _____

**Round 7:**

survey _____
tripod _____
level _____
transit _____
telescope _____

**Round 8:**

pencil _____
nail _____
microphone _____
spike _____
eye dropper _____
baster _____

Answers on pp. 166–167.

# Living in the Hearing World

Read the situation below, then watch the videotaped conversation "Living in the Hearing World." After you are able to follow the exchange, answer the questions that follow.

**Situation:** Sandra is relieved when her roommate Carlene finally gets home a few hours late from a Deaf bowling tournament in Las Vegas.

Sandra: } greetings
Carlene: }

Sandra:   expresses concern about Carlene's lateness, asks if the flight was delayed
Carlene:  expresses frustration, explains what happened at the airport:
  • she missed her flight
  • she had difficulty locating a TTY at the airport
  • the TTY wasn't working
Sandra:   responds, asks about her weekend in Las Vegas
Carlene:  talks about the weekend
Sandra:   asks if she saw a particular guy there (name sign T-on-shoulder)
Carlene:  says yes, but she didn't recognize him at first
Sandra:   responds
Carlene:  makes additional comments, mentions she saw Sandra's former boyfriend at the tournament
Sandra:   reacts
Carlene:  gives further information, then informs Sandra the phone is ringing
Sandra: } leavetakings...
Carlene: }

**1.** Why did Carlene miss her flight?


**2.** How did she locate the TTY at the airport? Where was it?


**3.** Why couldn't she use the TTY?


**4.** How did she inform her boyfriend about the delay?


**5.** How many people attended the event in Las Vegas?


**6.** Explain how Carlene recognized the man whose name sign is T-on-shoulder. What information does she give about him?


Answers on p. 167.

## Notes on the Conversation

**Accessibility**. The airport experiences Carlene describes happen all too often to many Deaf individuals. A Deaf person may miss a flight because s/he was not informed of an announcement. (Ticket agents often insist that the Deaf person sit and wait until the agent is free to assist him/her, and nearly as often the agent forgets. Usually if airline personnel inform the Deaf person of a change, that person can take care of the situation him/herself.) TTYs may not be readily accessible, either because airport personnel don't know where they are, or they are located in a distant area of the terminal, or they are stored at an information center that is closed at night. Sometimes the TTYs themselves are locked up, requiring the assistance of airport personnel to unlock them—an inconvenience when someone is in a hurry.

There are many tales about incidents like this, and not only at airports. More than once, well-meaning flight attendants have ordered wheelchairs to take Deaf passengers from one boarding gate to another during a flight change. Sometimes Deaf passengers are offered reading materials in Braille. Stories like these graphically illustrate the frustrations Deaf people encounter in the hearing world. The frustration is not because Deaf people can't hear, but because the hearing world is unaware of their needs. Ideally, ticket agents and airline attendants would be able to sign well. The next best thing would be if agents would *ask* Deaf people if they want assistance, rather than assume it's needed, and *inform* Deaf people, using paper and pencil, of what to expect.

## The Story Corner

### "Uncoding the Ethics"

Freda relates a joke about a hearing man who woke up one morning to find the bag of money he had hidden in his yard missing. When he saw footprints leading to the house of his Deaf neighbor, he knew who took his money. He brought a Sign Language interpreter with him, as well as his shotgun, to confront the neighbor. Watch what happens during the exchange between the neighbors with the interpreter as an intermediary.

Look in the Answer Key, p. 168, for a summary of the joke.

# LANGUAGE IN PERFORMANCE

## Legends

It is not uncommon to see a group of Deaf people gathered and held simply by the narrative of a story. What better story than one that idealizes the feats of Deaf people throughout history? These stories reaffirm the present by instilling meaning into the past. There are many such legends told throughout the Deaf community. By retelling these stories, the community develops a special shared knowledge essential to its existence.

**The Deaf Spies of the Civil War.** In his introduction to this piece, Sam Supalla explains that Ben will present a legend about Deaf people during the Civil War, a legend that has been passed on through the generations. This legend is about two Deaf soldiers, one who fought for the Union army and the other a Confederate.* They were each sent out to spy on the opposing army. They ran into each other, waited for a few moments in suspense, and when neither one spoke they each realized that the other was Deaf. In great relief, they set down their guns and ended up chatting all afternoon. After waiting for his spy's return, the Union captain finally sent out a search party. They found the two soldiers talking and assumed they were trading military secrets. The two soldiers were arrested and brought back for trial. The captain appealed to President Lincoln before passing judgment. Lincoln, who was preparing to sign the charter to found Gallaudet University, responded that the two soldiers demonstrated the true meaning of brotherhood, a concept otherwise devastated by the war.

This Civil War legend may be based on an actual incident, but is elaborated to emphasize the moral of the story, which is that political, religious and economic differences are superseded by the bonds shared by Deaf people. This story stresses the cultural value of solidarity among Deaf people, the idea that if they stick together, Deaf people will survive.

*End of Unit 17*

*Although currently Deaf people are classified as 4F, and therefore are not used as soldiers in the U.S. military, they were apparently permitted to fight during the Civil War. There is in fact a related legend about the 4F classification being established during the Civil War. According to the legend, an important general became frustrated with Deaf soldiers because of their lack of response to his speech, and in retaliation he set up the 4F classification. Another related legend Ben alludes to in this story is that the statue of Lincoln in the Lincoln Memorial has one hand in the A-handshape and the other in the L-handshape (Lincoln's initials) because the sculptor of the statue was the same one who created the statue of Gallaudet and Alice Cogswell, now on the grounds of Gallaudet University.

# Unit 17
## KEY PHRASES

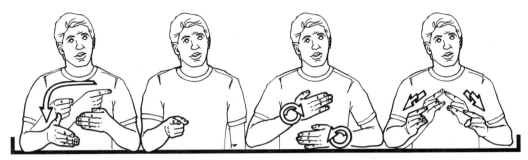

Ask person if she/he enjoyed camping over the weekend

Ask how the weekend was

Tell how your camping trip was cut-short

Tell what happened Friday night (arriving at a ski resort)

Tell what happened Saturday morning (skiing all morning)

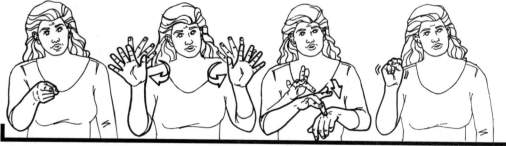

Ask if person has ever been to Seattle and ask what's there to see

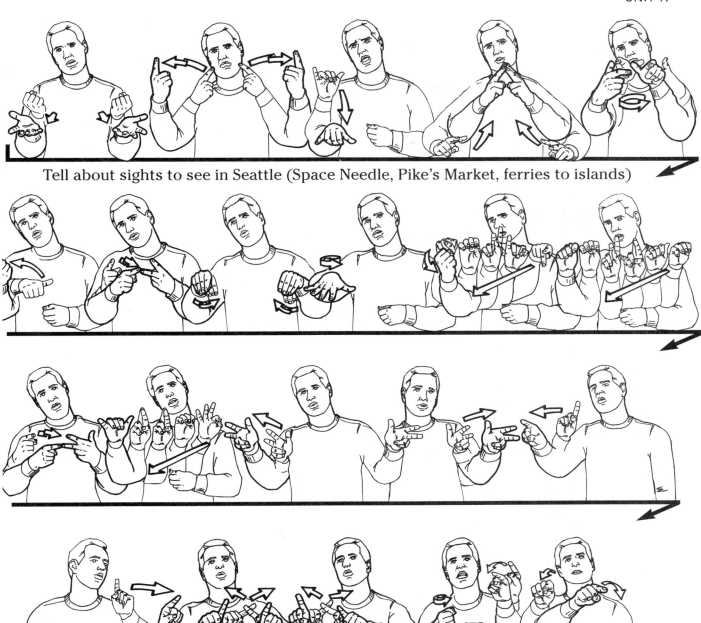

Tell about sights to see in Seattle (Space Needle, Pike's Market, ferries to islands)

# VOCABULARY REVIEW

FOUR SEASONS

WEEKEND ACTIVITIES

"taking-it-easy"
"biding time"

"busy as a bee"
doing errands
running errands

**RECREATION AND EXERCISE**

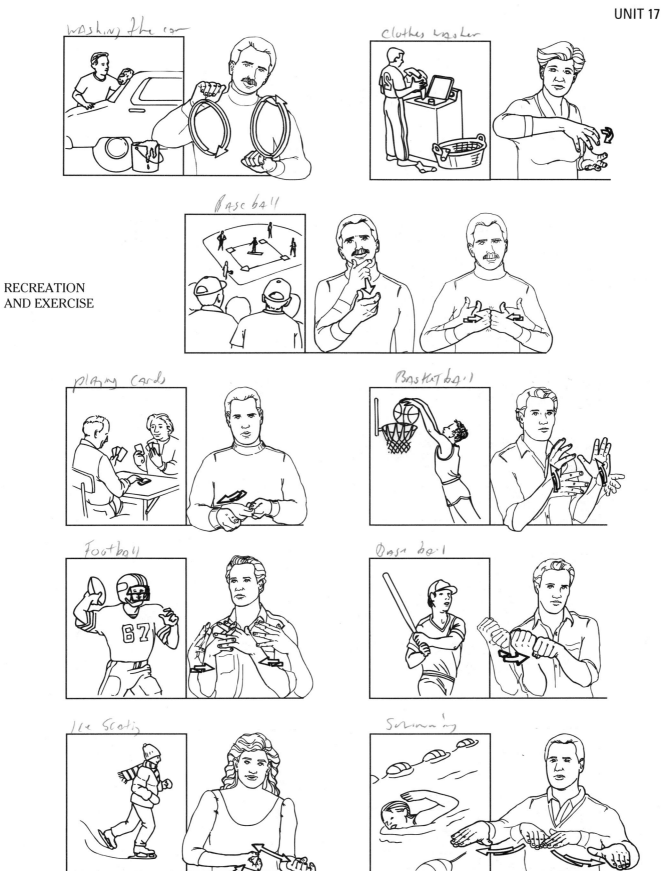

washing the car

clothes washer

Baseball

playing cards

Basketball

Football

base ball

Ice Skating

Swimming

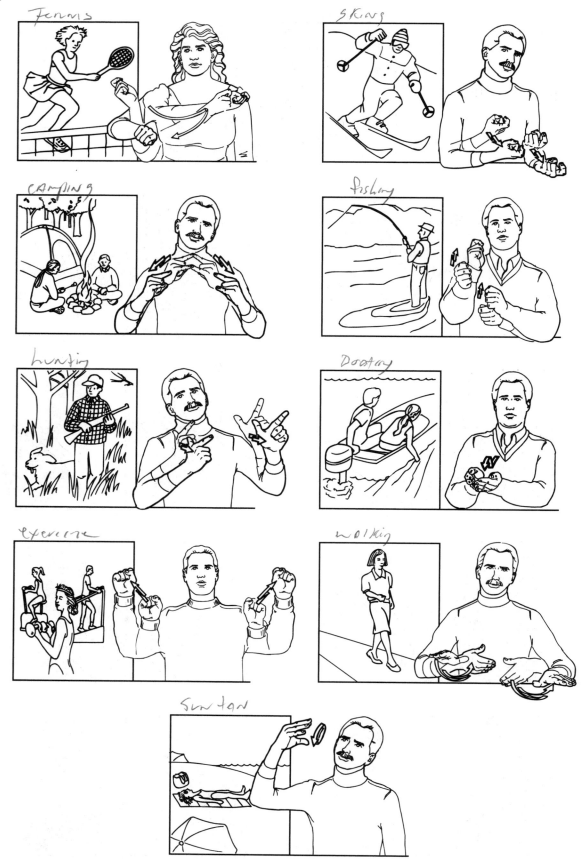

TASKS AROUND THE HOUSE

shoveling

planting

HOLIDAYS

easter

Halloween

Halloween

thanksgiving

Thanksgiving

Christmas

chaanukah

138

party

SPECIAL EVENTS

graduate

workshop

acting

parade

marriage

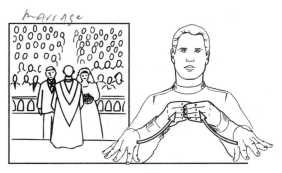

celebration

Tournament

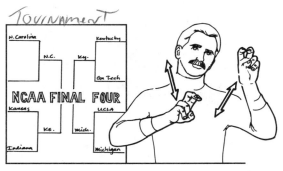

ferris wheel

CARNAVAL

CONTINUITY:
Durative time signs

PLANS DISRUPTED DUE
TO WEATHER

SNOWing

Raining

Windy

tornado

fog

**PLANS DISRUPTED DUE TO HEALTH PROBLEMS**

**PLANS DISRUPTED DUE TO CAR PROBLEMS**

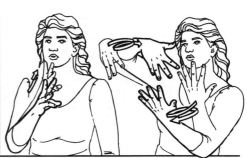

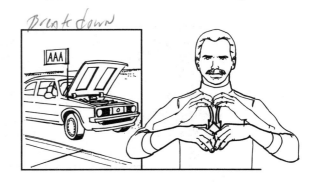

Broken into

accident

Flood

**PLANS DISRUPTED DUE
TO HOUSE PROBLEMS**

Water Leak

Break in

Fire

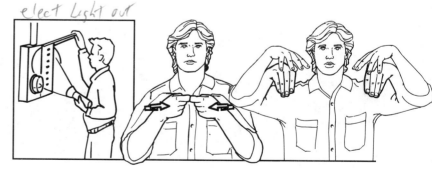

elect light out

**PLANS DISRUPTED DUE
TO PERSONAL REASONS**

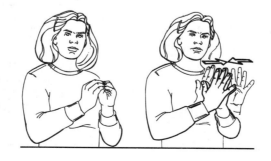

PLANS DISRUPTED DUE
TO WORK PROBLEMS

143

26
4
/104

## OPINIONS ABOUT ACTIVITIES

positive ———— negative

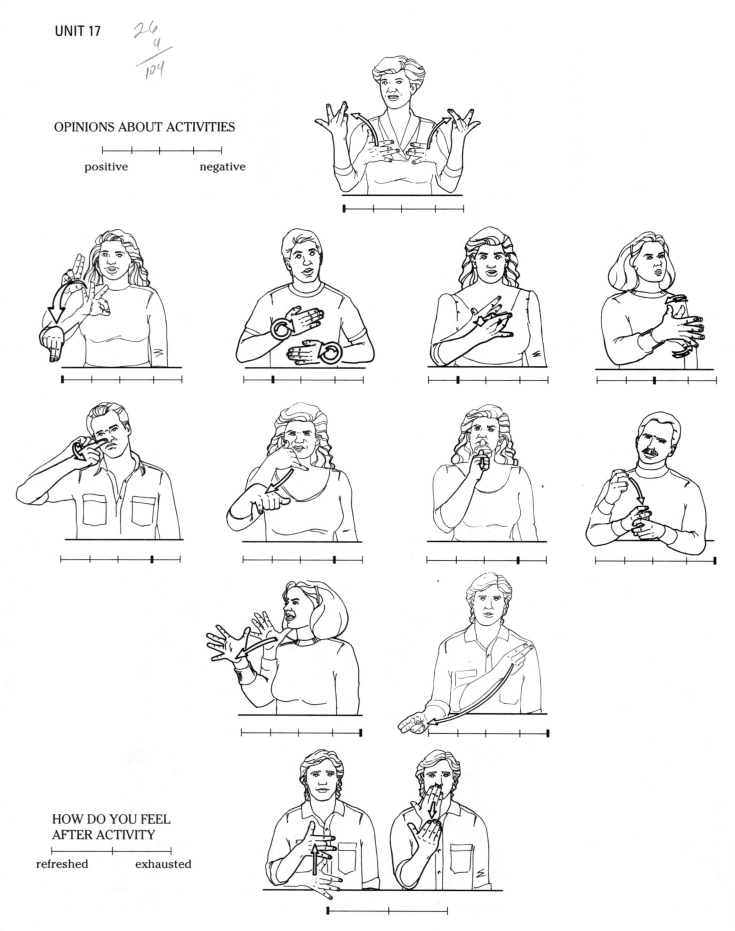

## HOW DO YOU FEEL
## AFTER ACTIVITY

refreshed ———— exhausted

144

FEELINGS ABOUT DISRUPTED PLANS

negative          positive

ORGANIZED/DISORGANIZED

# UNITS 13–17
## Cumulative Review

## LANGUAGE AND CULTURE

CULTURE NOTES

## Getting, Directing and Maintaining Attention

On screen you will see several scenes that focus on acceptable ways to get attention, direct someone's attention to another person, and maintain attention by controlling the pace of a conversation. Other scenes show how to resume a conversation after an interruption, and how to indicate that you're unsure how to spell a name.

When you are in a situation where distance or visibility prevents you from getting another person's attention, you may need someone else to help you get that person's attention. This intermediary person would either tap the one you want to talk to and point in your direction; tap the table and point in your direction; or, if the intermediary person already has the other's attention, simply point to you, or say "Lisa wants you" and point. In directing another person's attention it is important that you conclude by pointing to the person who wants the attention of the other.

When you want to get the attention of everyone in the room, begin by waving with one or both hands and scanning the room. As you make eye contact with different people, either ask them to look your way because you have something to say, or ask their help in directing others' attention to you. Making sure you have everyone's attention is appropriate behavior. To begin before you have everyone's attention is considered thoughtless and disruptive. Once everyone is looking your way, make your announcement. Make eye contact with everyone in the room as you address the group to be sure you include everyone.

Observe the attention-getting behaviors used in various situations. The assumption is that everyone in these scenes is acquainted—attention-getting behaviors would differ in more formal situations.

### Directing the attention of one person to another

**Scene 1**: Mary waves to get Ivanetta's attention; Ivanetta taps Yolanda, gives Mary's name, then points to Mary.

**Scene 2**: Priscilla taps the table to get Dan's attention; Dan waves to get Cinnie's attention, then points to Priscilla.

**Scene 3**: Mary waves to get Carlene's attention; Carlene interrupts the conversation with the gesture "wait a second" so she can see what Mary wants; then Carlene informs Yolanda that Mary wants her, and finally points to Mary.

**Getting attention from outside the group**

**Scene 4**: Bob comes in quietly, stoops down, taps Cinnie, hands her a note and explains it's a message.

**Scene 5:** Lon approaches, leans down and waves to Ethan, asks a question quickly, and explains where he can be found.

**Getting the attention of everyone in the group**

**Scene 6**: Cinnie gets the attention of the chairperson by raising her hand, then gets the attention of the group by explaining she wants to make an announcement; she scans the group to make eye contact with each person while making her announcement.

**Scene 7**: Pat taps the people close by and asks their assistance in getting others' attention; she waves to get the attention of people further away and asks their assistance also; she scans the room to be sure everyone's eyes are on her, then makes her announcement.

## Controlling the Pace of Conversation

On screen you will see Mary and Cinnie demonstrate how to maintain a conversation while the listener is busy doing something.

The listener uses quick glances away at appropriate times to minimize interruptions, nods to signal the signer to continue, or in instances of prolonged interruptions, holds up one finger to ask the signer to wait a second.

The signer accommodates the listener by holding a sign, slowing down a sign, repeating a sign, and adjusting her position to make it easier for the listener to see the signer and continue with what she's doing.

Now watch Mary and Cinnie demonstrate listener and signer strategies for controlling the pace of the conversation. We show clips of their conversations in slow motion so that you can clearly see the different strategies they use.

## Resuming the Conversation

On screen you will see signers use different strategies to resume a conversation after an interruption. The phrases used will vary, depending on how the conversation is resumed. Watch each scene and see if you can pick out the different phrases used to resume the conversation.

**Scene 1**: Ethan resumes the conversation by recalling where he left off.
**Scene 2**: Sandra continues the conversation where she left off.
**Scene 3**: Ethan prompts Priscilla to finish her story by repeating the last thing she said.
**Scene 4**. Anthony asks Ivanetta where he left off, and she reminds him of the topic.
**Scene 5**: Carlene asks Mary what she was saying before the interruption, then continues.

Practice the phrases used to resume a conversation after an interruption.

## Getting Help with Spelling of Names

On screen you will see dialogues where a person is identified by name. Pay particular attention to the phrases highlighted below.

### Dialogue 1

*Mary*: explains she just met a woman who knows Steve, describes the woman, **says her name is J- something**

*Steve*: asks if she is from Chicago, spells name, describes further to confirm

*Mary*: **confirms**, relays message

### Dialogue 2

*Ramona*: asks if Shane knows (gives name sign), spells first name, **says last name is G-something**

*Shane*: asks if she's short

*Ramona*: confirms

*Shane*: spells last name

*Ramona*: **corrects**, adds more description

*Shane*: spells different name

*Ramona*: **says name seems correct**

## PAIR PRACTICE

Practice the phrases by role playing with a partner. Follow this dialogue format:

> *A:* describe a person, ask for help with spelling the name
> *B:* spell name
> *A:* respond

Possible people and things to describe:

- someone from your class, or a well-known person on campus
- a famous person such as an actor, the President of the U.S., a sports figure
- an object such as an appliance, tool or piece of clothing
- a brand-name product

# LANGUAGE IN PRACTICE

## Confirming Questions

On screen you will see three different signs used to ask confirming questions. The first two examples use this sign. It is used when you are quite certain your information is correct, but you want to confirm it.

The next two examples use this sign. It is used when you have heard a rumor or think you have the right information, and want to check it out with someone who may know.

**G R A M M A R N O T E S**

The last six examples use this sign. It is used for a number of reasons:

- you are unsure about doing something and want to ask another person's opinion
- you present a hypothetical situation and ask if it is true, or if it could happen that way
- you are curious about some information and want to know if the other person agrees

Now watch the videotaped demonstrations of each type of confirming sign. Pay particular attention to the facial expressions used while asking confirming questions.

**Check if the information is correct:**
Example 1: The founder of Gallaudet University was hearing.
Example 2: Armstrong was the first person to walk on the moon.

**Check if the rumors are true:**
Example 1: The next Sign Language class session will be cancelled.
Example 2: President Bush's grandson is deaf.

**Check another person's opinion:**
Example 1: It's all right to drink tap water in Mexico.
Example 2: It's worthwhile to attend the workshop.

**Check if a hypothetical situation could be true:**
Example 1: If you wait a few weeks to buy your airline ticket, the fare will go up.
Example 2: If you put a tooth under your pillow, the toothfairy will replace it with a quarter.

**Check if the other person agrees:**
Example 1: A certain restaurant will be open on Sunday.
Example 2: Tomorrow's meeting will be interpreted.

Replay the segment and practice asking confirming questions.

## Which Number Was That?

Shane, Mary, Steve, and Sandra will sign 12 numbers or phrases with both a number and fingerspelled word. Circle the corresponding item below.

| | | | |
|---|---|---|---|
| **1.** $2.50 | **4.** June 7, 1938 | **7.** 1:15 | **10.** 202 Ella |
| 2:50 | Jan. 7, 1938 | 1:05 | 200 Vella |
| 12:50 | Jan. 8, 1938 | 115 | 22 Vella |
| | | | |
| **2.** 101 | **5.** 1570s | **8.** 3 | **11.** 21 London |
| 111 | 1480s | $3.00 | 21 Londen |
| $1.01 | 1520s | 3:00 | 21 Ondon |
| | | | |
| **3.** Nov. 22, 1992 | **6.** 10¢ | **9.** 479 Freider | **12.** 36 Walden |
| Nov. 2, 1992 | 10 yrs. old | 479 Reider | 3 Walden |
| Nov. 12, 1992 | 10:00 | 47 Freider | 36 Alden |

Answers on p. 168.

# Questions to Ask and Statements to Make

Now that you are at the end of Level 2, you should be able to ask the following questions or make the following statements. Read the cues for each item, think about how you would sign it, then watch the signers model the sentences on screen.

1. Ask what color the outside of the house is.

2. Ask someone where s/he keeps magazines.

3. Tell someone that the living room is to the right as you enter the house.

4. Ask if most homes in that area have two bedrooms.

5. Tell someone that the appliances in your kitchen (stove, refrigerator and dishwasher) are all of different colors.

6. Ask someone if s/he has a weakness for candy.

7. Tell a person s/he doesn't look happy; ask what's the matter.

8. Ask someone if s/he'll let you sit in the antique rocking chair.

9. Ask someone how s/he enjoyed her first trip to Europe.

10. Tell someone you're sick of your brother tattling to your mom every time you argue. (Hint: use a when clause.)

11. Ask someone how many weddings s/he has attended.

12. Ask a person why s/he detests playing golf.

13. Tell someone that your friend's mother and her sister married two brothers.

14. Tell someone that Jenna's parents have five deaf children, and that her aunt and uncle have four deaf children.

15. Ask someone what "deja vu" means.

16. Ask someone if s/he has a cheese grater. (Hint: describe the grater.)

17. Ask if tacos are very spicy. (Hint: describe a taco.)

18. Ask a person if s/he prefers eggs boiled, scrambled, fried, or poached.

19. Ask how much that furry cushion costs.

20. Tell someone that work was hell this week.

21. Tell a person that someone forgot to bring charcoal to last night's barbecue party, which messed the whole thing up.

22. Ask someone if s/he likes to take it easy or keep busy in his/her spare time.

23. Tell someone that during the 1920s people rebelled against prohibition, drank, partied, and had a good time, until the Depression hit in the 1930s, leaving many people stunned.

Write the cued questions and statements on index cards. Then find a partner and take turns asking or telling each other what's on the cards. Give appropriate responses.

## The Story Corner

**"We Got Plenty of Them Back Home"**

Ben Bahan relates a joke about three passengers on a train: a Russian, a Cuban, and a Deaf man. Watch the exchange that follows and answer what it is that each of them got plenty of back home.

Russian: _____

Cuban: _____

Deaf man: _____

Answers on p. 168.

# LANGUAGE IN PERFORMANCE

## Drama

Many forms of drama have long been popular in the Deaf community. At residential schools for the Deaf, children frequently imitate houseparents and teachers to entertain each other in the dorms. Those who become talented actors and storytellers may later get involved in collaborative presentations such as skits and school plays, as well as performances at Literary Society meetings. Some continue to use these skills in college plays or entertainment at Deaf clubs and community events. Freda Norman was such a child, demonstrating talents very early. She has pursued a career in acting that has involved her in a number of professional theatre groups, including the National Theatre of the Deaf.

**Monologue.** Sam Supalla introduces Freda's performance of this segment of Rico Peterson's play, *Seeing Place*. In this monologue an age-old question is asked— Is Sign Language a real language? Is it possible for a visual-gestural language to have a highly articulated grammatical structure? Can a language without a written form communicate complex ideas and abstract thought? Is it possible that a visual-gestural language exhibits the same linguistic properties as spoken languages? For those of us who have firsthand experience with ASL and the Deaf community, it is easy to answer the question with a definite YES! But frequently for the rest of the world, the question still needs an answer.

In this scene, all languages are represented as children learning their own language. And like children, they can be very cruel when faced with something different than themselves. As Baby ASL is growing and learning about her language and the world around her, she is confronted and taunted by the other languages. Out of ignorance she is excluded as an "inferior" language. Baby ASL seeks the answer from Mother Tongue.

*End of Cumulative Review: Units 13–17*

# CR Units 13–17
## KEY PHRASES

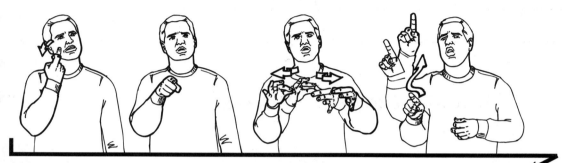

Ask another person to resume story by repeating what was last said

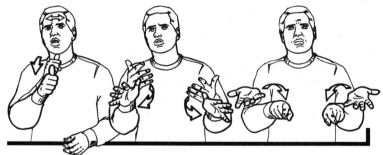

Ask for help in resuming conversation

Resume conversation by yourself

Check if information is correct

Check if rumor is true

Check another person's opinion

## UNIT 13
## Describing the Layout of a Home

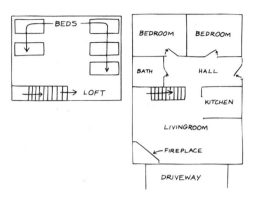

## Describing the Arrangement of a Room

Room Description 1

Room Description 2

Room Description 3

Room Description 4

# Locating Small Objects

## Minidialogue 1

1. the electric bill
2. a) in the kitchen
   b) next to the window
   c) in the cupboard
   d) on the top shelf
3. family

## Minidialogue 2

1. his camera
2. a) in the bedroom
   b) in the dresser
   c) in the bottom drawer
   d) on the left side
3. he asks if she means the dresser with the mirror
4. family

## Minidialogue 3

1. nailclippers
2. a) in the bathroom
   b) near the bathtub
   c) in the basket
3. in the sink
4. family

## Minidialogue 4

1. a dictionary
2. a) in the living room
   b) on the table
   c) in the stack of books
3. the one in front of the couch
4. friends

# Where Do You Keep It?

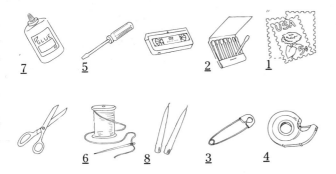

# Rearrangements and Renovations

## Dialogue 1

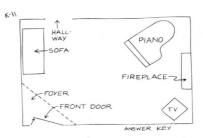

## Dialogue 2

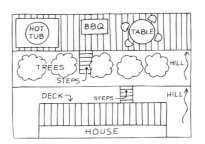

## Dialogue 3

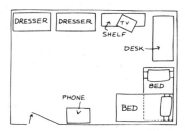

## Dialogue 4

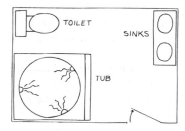

## Number Practice

| number | topic |
|---|---|
| 1. $600 | cost of dresser |
| 2. 105 | page number of book |
| 3. 104 | candies in jar |
| 4. 102 | grandmother's age |
| 5. 107 | office number |
| 6. 100 | temperature everyday the past week |
| 7. 300 | people at meeting |
| 8. 800 | phone number for information |
| 9. 400 | miles from here to Chicago |
| 10. 1,000 | people who bought tickets |

## Fingerspelling: Double-Letter Words

1. attic
2. Jeannette
3. hill
4. class
5. all, TTY
6. cotton
7. free
8. weeds
9. burrito
10. flannel sheets

## Where's a Good Place to Shop?

1. that he bought a new house
2. to ask about a good place to buy materials for remodeling

3. Lumber
   Moldings
   Masonry
   Paint
   Doors
   Windows
   Bathroom Fixtures
   Tools
   Kitchen Cabinets

4.

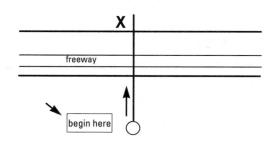

## The Story Corner: "Exploring a Cave"

They were in the cave all day and all night because they were lost.

# UNIT 14

## Asking to Borrow a Truck

| type of response | explanation/suggestion |
|---|---|
| Joe: decline, tell why | the truck belongs to the company and he is not allowed to let others use it |
| Shane: decline, suggest other solution | his brother is using his truck for a week, so suggests he contact Pat |
| Pat: hedge | her truck isn't reliable |
| Cinnie: agree, tell shortcoming | the bed of the truck is filthy after hauling a greasy engine |
| Lon: agree, with condition | the gas tank is almost empty, so Anthony would have to fill it up |

## Inflections for Temporal Aspect

1. recurring
2. uninflected
3. recurring
4. continuous
5. uninflected
6. recurring
7. continuous
8. recurring
9. continuous
10. continuous
11. uninflected
12. recurring
13. uninflected
14. recurring
15. continuous
16. uninflected
17. continuous
18. recurring

## Making Requests

### Dialogue 1
1. That Cinnie go to the pharmacy to pick up Tina Jo's medicine.
2. The pharmacy closes in 15 minutes, but she is busy cooking.
3. Most pharmacies require identification to pick up prescription medicines, unless the pick-up is prearranged.
4. Cinnie will help with the cooking while Tina Jo goes to the pharmacy.

### Dialogue 2
1. If the cabinets could be installed on Saturday.
2. He can't this Saturday, but can do it the following Saturday.
3. Carlene's parents-in-law are coming next Wednesday, so she would like to have the cabinets installed by then.
4. Lon will ask a friend to install the cabinets for him.

### Dialogue 3
1. To meet Anthony at 11:00 a.m. instead of 2:00 p.m. that day.
2. He can't make it by 11 because he needs to shower and change.
3. To postpone the meeting to the next day.
4. To meet at 3:00 p.m. the next day.

### Dialogue 4
1. To show her the work he just finished.
2. Because she already left in her car.
3. To call Pat and inform her that Lon will stop by her place later in the evening to show her his work.

## Clock Numbers Practice

| number(s) | topic |
|---|---|
| 1. 1:17 | time of birth |
| 2. 5:13 | 1906 San Francisco earthquake |
| 3. 7:35 | game starting time |
| 4. 9:52 | arrival time of flight |
| 5. 6:49 | next bus |
| 6. 3:13 to 3:28 | length of break |
| 7. 12:19, 12:36 | time of birth of twins |
| 8. 7:26, 8:05, 8:37 | train schedule |

## Fingerspelling: Common Fingerspelled Words

1. flu, stiff
2. cut, hurt
3. foot, nail
4. rent, own
5. condo, sale
6. Ave., or, Blvd.
7. roof, tile, door
8. Toyota, van, used
9. car, clutch, safe
10. Honda, Civic, gas, m.p.g.

## The Fortune Teller

*Mary's complaint*: her dog buries one of her shoes in the yard every morning

*Advice*: pour concrete in the yard
*Reaction*: she thinks it's great advice

*Anthony's complaint*: when he babysits, his younger brothers play around when they are supposed to be sleeping, but he hasn't been able to catch them at it

*Advice*: install a window in the ceiling so he can see the kids' bedroom from downstairs
*Reaction*: he likes the advice and plans to tell his parents about it

*Dan's complaint*: water is leaking from the ceiling in the garage

*First advice*: don't give his wife any money, but keep it himself
*Second advice*: make the fence higher so the neighbors won't be able to peer in
*Reaction*: complete frustration—he thinks she's a lousy fortune teller

She can only give advice about problems with pets, children, spouse/roommate, or neighbors.

*Bonus*: TILT!

## The Story Corner: "Final Exam"

The student stuck his paper in the middle of the stack so the professor couldn't identify it.

## Cheers and Songs

The song is "The Star-Spangled Banner."

# UNIT 15

## Discussing Nationalities

Cinnie's father is Norwegian.
Cinnie's mother is German, Irish and French.
Cinnie's husband's name is Irish.
Tina Jo thought Cinnie was Polish.
Tina Jo's mother's nationality is French, Italian and Swiss, among others.
Tina Jo's father is half German and half Russian.

## Cinnie's Biographical Sketch

This is a translation of Cinnie's narrative:

*Birth:* I was born in Sacramento, California in 1956.

*Family:* My family is all Deaf. I have two brothers, and I am the second child in the family.

*School:* At five years of age, I enrolled at the California School for the Deaf in Berkeley. In my senior year, I took the Gallaudet Entrance Examinations and passed.

*First college:* After graduation, I attended Gallaudet. During my junior year, I realized I had been in the Deaf world all my life. I wanted to see what the hearing world was like.

*Second college:* So I decided to withdraw from Gallaudet and return to California, where I attended a state university. It was a very different experience having to rely on Sign Language interpreters in the classroom. It was like having three-way communication. At Gallaudet, the teachers communicated directly with us, which I preferred.

The following fall, I returned to Gallaudet. Upon graduation, I came back to California, but I couldn't get work teaching Deaf children because I didn't have a master's degree. Then I thought about something I've always wanted to do—join the Peace Corps. They don't require a master's degree, so I applied.

*Peace Corps assignment:* I was offered a teaching assignment in the Philippines, and I accepted. I tried to persuade my boyfriend to join me in the Peace Corps, but he didn't want to, which was fine with me.

In the spring of 1979, I started work at a School for the Deaf in the Philippines. Near the end of my two-year assignment, my boyfriend decided he wanted to join me in the Peace Corps, so I extended my stay. After he finished his two-year stint, the two of us began our travels around the world.

*Travels after the Peace Corps:* First we flew to Thailand and stayed there two weeks. Then we travelled to India, stayed there four days, then on to Italy for two weeks. After Italy, we flew to Paris, then took the train to Austria, Germany, Holland, Brussels, then back to Paris, where we took a flight to England for the flight back to America.

*First job back in the U.S.:* After arriving in New York, I looked for a job and got a position as assistant teacher at the American School for the Deaf in Hartford, Connecticut. I worked there for six months.

*Wedding:* In the summer of 1983, my boyfriend and I got married here in California and then decided to move out here.

*Jobs in California:* My husband got a job at the California School for the Deaf in Fremont, and I taught ASL at Vista College in the evenings. In the daytime, I had a job teaching Deaf-Blind people.

After two years, I left my job and got another position teaching job seeking skills to Deaf adults, which I held for a year. However, the agency folded and I was laid off.

*Graduate school:* I decided to attend the master's program in Deaf Education at San Francisco State University, where I have been for the past three years.

*Husband's career change:* Last year my husband left his job at the School for the Deaf to work with a Deaf publishing company.

*Current plans:* Later, the company decided to relocate to San Diego. Meanwhile, I finished my studies and got pregnant. So we both decided to move to San Diego. We have bought a house there and the baby is due sometime in October.

We might eventually settle down.

## Telling About Unexpected Changes

### Situation 1
*What happened:* she was laid off, so had to return here and move back in with her parents

### Situation 2
*What happened:* his wife got sick, he had to stay home to tend to her

### Situation 3
*What happened:* he fell off a rope swing, broke his leg, has been using crutches for four months

### Situation 4
*What happened:* after turning on the heat to warm the house, she drifted off again, overslept, then went to get coffee and ran into a friend

## The Immigrants

1. great-grandfather
2. father
3. grandmother
4. great-grandmother

## Number Practice

| number | topic |
|--------|-------|
| 1. 119 | room number for the meeting |
| 2. 111 | temperature of hot tub |
| 3. 117 | number of new houses on lot |
| 4. 113 | winning team's total points |
| 5. 110 | horsepower of car engine |
| 6. 115 | average bowling score |
| 7. 112 | miles round trip to work |
| 8. 118 | weight of dog |
| 9. 114 | page number for homework |
| 10. 116 | winning number |

## Dates and Addresses

### Specific Dates

| | |
|---|---|
| Date first Deaf president of Gallaudet University selected | March 17, 1989 |
| Laurent Clerc's birthdate | December 26, 1785 |
| Douglas Tilden's birthdate | May 1, 1860 |
| Founding of the American School for the Deaf | April 15, 1817 |

### Periods of Time

| | |
|---|---|
| Wave of immigration to America from northern Europe | 1870s and 1880s |
| Era of Deaf performers in silent films | 1910s and 1920s |
| Years that captioned films were popular | 1960s and 1970s |
| Boom of Deaf workers in the war industry | 1940s |

### Span of Years

| | |
|---|---|
| Life of Laura Searing | 1840–1923 |
| Years Germany was divided into East and West | 1945–1990 |
| Years Edward M. Gallaudet served as college president | 1864–1910 |
| The building of the Golden Gate Bridge | 1933–1937 |

### Addresses

517 Third St.
2796 Michigan Ave.
38485 LaSalle Blvd.
92074 (zip code)

## A Show of Hands

1. Mark: works at the Bank of Japan exchanging foreign currencies.
   Liz: Svetla is a Russian name. Liz works for a travel agency. (She mentions that Australia and Greece were popular travel destinations last year, but that Holland and Egypt are currently very popular.)
2. Name two countries where ASL is used.
3. U.S. and Canada
4. Where was he born? (Note: The Abbe de l'Epée founded the first school for the Deaf in France in the mid-1700s.)
5. France
6. Italy, Japan, Israel
7. Brazil, New Zealand, Switzerland, and Czechoslovakia
8. Austria, Poland, Switzerland, Germany
9. Greece
10. Czechoslovakia and Iraq
11. Cheese from Norway, wine from Italy, a watch from Switzerland
12. A two-week trip for two to England, all expenses paid
13. Mark

## It's a Small World

1. Pat is her former houseparent at the School for the Deaf
2. yes — she has one year till her retirement
3. they're in college together
4. Ohio
5. they have the same last name
6. California
7. Clyde's father
8. yes
9. for a high-paying job in a rubber factory
10. Pat's sister; Gallaudet
11. from Gallaudet
12. he has passed away; his daughter doesn't sign well, but has a deaf grandson
13. public school
14. they have been been learning to sign, and now sign well
15. because it's time for the raffle drawing

## The Story Corner: "The Dead Dog"

When the owner came to pick up her dog, she knew it wasn't hers: her dog was dead when she checked in for the flight.

# UNIT 16

## Have Clock, Will Travel

first model

second model

electronic display
folds up
is put under pillow so
    person can feel alarm
    vibrate
battery operated
    (implied)
$28.

bulky
has clock face (analog)
alarm signals flashing
light
battery operated
$35.

## Describing Objects

1.

|  |  |
|---|---|
| identify object: | vase |
| identify color: | white |
| identify size: | a little over a foot tall |
| describe basic shape: | cylinder |
| describe details: | spiral design |
| perspective used: | no front |
| type of sequence: | not fixed |

2.

|  |  |
|---|---|
| identify object: | L.A. Rams football helmet |
| describe basic shape: | spherical |
| describe details: | face mask, logo on side, chin strap |
| perspective used: | on body |
| type of sequence: | not fixed |

3.

|  |  |
|---|---|
| identify object: | hanging lamp |
| identify material: | metal cover, glass shade |
| describe basic shape: | dome and conical |
| describe details: | translucent glass shade with ridges, pull-cord |
| perspective used: | neutral space |
| type of sequence: | fixed: from ceiling down |

4.

|  |  |
|---|---|
| identify object: | old stove |
| dentify material: | metal |
| describe basic shape: | box-like |
| describe details: | metal claws on bottom, six gas burners, six knobs, large oven, broiler on left side, two storage compartments on bottom, warming oven on top |
| perspective used: | from the front |
| type of sequence: | fixed: top to bottom |

5.

|  |  |
|---|---|
| identify object: | couch |
| describe basic shape: | rectangular, (soft) |
| identify color/pattern: | blue and white striped |
| describe details: | recliner on right side |
| perspective used: | from the front, then from sitting position |
| type of sequence: | fixed: abstracted |

6.

|  |  |
|---|---|
| identify object: | camcorder |
| describe basic shape: | rectangular |
| identify size: | standard size, about a foot long |
| describe details: | viewfinder, on/off switch, buttons on side to input date, buttons on top for zoom, button to open cassette compartment, button to replay footage just filmed |
| perspective used: | from the rear |
| type of sequence: | not fixed |

7.

|  |  |
|---|---|
| identify object: | tent |
| describe basic shape: | dome |
| describe details: | held up by assembled poles, tabs on outside for the poles, door with zipper, sleeps three people, small window at rear with zipper |
| perspective used: | from the front |
| type of sequence: | fixed: top to bottom |

## Picture It

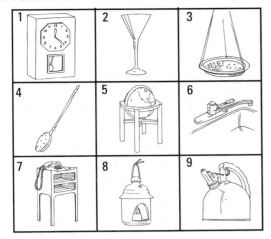

## Potpourri

### Minidialogue 1

### Minidialogue 2
edger

### Minidialogue 3

### Minidialogue 4
chopped chicken; red, green and yellow bell peppers sauteed in butter; tortillas

### Minidialogue 5
One plant has a flower, the other has longer leaves and is located in the corner of the bedroom.

### Minidialogue 6
Needlepoint is done on a tightly woven canvas backing, while rug hooking is done on loosely woven canvas that provides a harder backing. Needlepoint is done with a needle and thread (or fine yarn) while rug hooking is done with a latchhook and short strands of yarn.

## What's a Sashimi?

1. Sashimi is raw tuna or salmon, with rice served separately. Sushi is raw fish on rice.
2. Ivanetta says sukiyaki is similar to soup.
3. Tempura is shrimp and vegetables dipped in flour, then deep fried in oil.

## Matching Costs with Objects

## History of TTYs

1. Without phones to contact friends, Deaf people had to travel by public transportation or by car to see their friends and families.

2. **1960s:** When Western Union Telegraph was getting rid of their old teletypewriters, a Deaf man invented a coupler that would allow Deaf people to use the teletypewriters to call each other. They had continuous paper printouts that were about ten inches wide.

   **1970:** Small portable devices known as teletypewriters came on the market. They had digital readouts but no paper printouts.

   **1975:** Printers were added to these devices. The printouts were about two inches wide.

   **1981**: In California a law was passed to mandate distribution of free TDDs to Deaf phone-company customers. This enabled a wider segment of the Deaf population to get in touch with each other easily.

   **1990:** Even smaller devices that could be easily carried around, i.e., in a pocket, came on the market.

3. They took up a lot of space in the house, were very noisy and were painted an unattractive green.

4. When the machine stopped shaking, Pat knew the person on the other end of the line had stopped typing.

5. They are lightweight and very convenient to carry around. In addition, they have a memory for storing phone numbers.

# UNIT 17

## Places to See in Seattle

1. Space Needle: It's a famous landmark with a revolving restaurant. It is expensive, but the food is delicious, and the view superb.

   Opinion: He likes it.

2. Pike's Market: There are many small specialty stores, including imports, crafts, antiques and items that are hard to find.

   Opinion: It's nice, a popular spot, but he doesn't really care for it.

3. Ferry to Victoria: It takes six hours and costs $25 per person (without a car). Earlier Lon mentioned the beautiful gardens.

   Opinion: It's worth it.

## The Signing Weekend

transitions

| | |
|---|---|
| 1. 00:27 | 5. 01:05–06 |
| 2. 00:35 | 6. 01:26–27 |
| 3. 00:41 | 7. 01:39 |
| 4. 00:47 | 8. 02:12 |

## Beginning Conversations

### Dialogue 1

1. Friday: Anthony's parents arrived in Los Angeles by surprise. Anthony picked them up, brought them home, and they chatted late into the night.

   Saturday: Anthony took his parents on a tour of Los Angeles including downtown, Hollywood and the beach.

   Sunday:  Anthony took his parents out to a restaurant and to go shopping. Then he dropped them off at the airport. He didn't have a chance to do the assignment.

2. Ethan asked Anthony to explain why he didn't get the assignment done.

### Dialogue 2

1. Friday: Sandra and her husband bought seeds and three tomato plants.

   Saturday: In the morning, her husband rototilled, raked and levelled the ground. In the afternoon they planted five rows of seeds and the three tomato plants, and put up wire fencing to hold the tomato plants upright. Then they watered the garden thoroughly.

   Sunday: They  watered the garden again.

2. Yolanda asked Sandra about her garden.

### Dialogue 3

1. Friday: Ethan's son took a bath and left the water running all night.

   Saturday: Ethan woke up to find the bathroom, the hallway and bedrooms flooded. He was very upset. He vacuumed and mopped the water up.

2. When Ethan arrived obviously upset, Joe asked him what was wrong. Ethan replied that his plans to go camping were cancelled, making Joe ask why.

## Dialogue 4

1. Friday: Mary and her husband flew down to Los Angeles and stayed overnight in the city.

   Saturday: They boarded a cruise ship and rode most of the day till they arrived at Catalina Island, then boarded a taxi boat to go from the cruise ship to the island. They toured the island, shopped, rented a golf cart and visited historical sites. Then they went back to the ship to sunbathe and change into formal wear. They returned to the island to eat at a fancy restaurant. It was wonderful and romantic. They spent the night on the ship.

   Sunday: They rode back to Los Angeles, visited some friends, then flew back home.

2. Tina Jo commented on how happy Mary seemed. Mary replied that she went to Catalina Island, which prompted Tina Jo to ask for more information about her trip.

## Dialogue 5

1. Saturday: Yolanda went to Long Beach with friends for a multicultural carnival. There were different foods, clothing, music and dance from Africa, Jamaica, Trinidad and the West Indies. In the evening the kids went on rides, then they all had delicious Jamaican food for dinner. It was late when Yolanda dropped her friends off at their home, then she had a long drive back home herself. By the time she arrived she was too tired and it was too late to go to the party.

2. Anthony asked Yolanda why she didn't show up at the party last Saturday. She responded by explaining her busy day.

## Disrupted Plans

### Narrative 1

1. At first the water was calm, but it became increasingly rough as the boat went further out.
2. She got seasick from watching the rolling waves, and threw up.
3. He decided to turn back because the water was too rough.
4. They got their money back.
5. She was disappointed about not going fishing, but accepted it.
6. back

### Narrative 2

1. It was outside on a sunny day. There was a canopy and lots of beautiful flowers.
2. The bride twisted her ankle and almost fell on her way down the aisle, but her father caught her in time.
3. The fan belt was missing so the car wouldn't start.
4. The groom got a fan belt from a friend and installed it.
5. A guest accidentally spilled red wine on the groom's white clothes while he was in the car getting ready to leave.
6. They thought the wedding was lovely, but so many things happened.
7. groom, VW, and belt.

### Narrative 3

1. They decided to build an addition (a family room) to their house.
2. They ordered the lumber to be delivered to their house.
3. Because she works on Fridays. She was supposed to take care of their daughter while her husband handled the arrival of the lumber.
4. Her husband said he could handle the delivery and keep an eye on the daughter, and it went well.
5. Because they saw on the news that it might rain that night.
6. It only drizzled.
7. Her husband got the flu.
8. He got better and the addition was completed, much to her satisfaction.
9. co (short for company), OK, TV, news, tarp, flu

### Narrative 4

1. An electrical problem. (If so, it could wait till he got to the next town.)
2. The engine overheated because the fan belt broke.
3. He found an extra fan belt in the trunk of his car and installed it.
4. The gas gauge didn't work, so he had no warning.
5. He got a ride to town to get some gas and got another ride back to the car.
6. Very late that night.
7. fan belt, tools, it, gas

**Narrative 5**

1. They found out that one tent pole was missing.
2. They used a stick instead of the pole.
3. It rained.
4. They decided to go ahead and hike in the rain.
5. To clean off the mud that covered them.
6. Yes. It was a beautiful day.
7. The friend drove the car to the end of the trail and Malcolm hiked alone up to the top of the mountain and then down to meet his friend.
8. pole, stick, mud

## Number Practice

| number(s) | topic |
|---|---|
| 1. $260 | how much she paid for two new tires |
| 2. 512 | amount of computer memory (512K) |
| 3. $368 | two-night package trip to Disneyland |
| 4. $540, $555 | amount of old rent and new rent |
| 5. $999, $789 | original price of a couch and how much she paid for it on sale |
| 6. 230, 190 | number of pounds Bill used to weigh and what he weighs now |
| 7. 888, 879 | number of votes counted for each candidate |
| 8. 444, 487 | number of people attending the play on Friday and Saturday nights |

## Descriptionary: A Game Show

**Round 1:**

**Round 2:**

**Round 3:**

**Round 4:**

**Round 5:**

**Round 6:**

**Round 7:**

**Round 8:**

**Round 1:**

| | |
|---|---|
| pinwheel | 4 |
| wheelbarrow | 1 |
| brace | 3 |
| edger | 2 |
| spur | 5 |

**Round 2:**

| | |
|---|---|
| coffee rack | 5 |
| driftwood | 1 |
| hat rack | 2 |
| pipes | 3 |
| deadwood | 5 |
| branches | 4 |
| carafe | 1 |
| cactus | 3 |

| Round 3: | | |
|---|---|---|
| | wedge | 3 |
| | ice cream maker | 2 |
| | butcher block | 3 |
| | birdbath | 4 |
| | cardholder | 1 |
| | cake | 5 |
| | sundial | 2 |

| Round 4: | | |
|---|---|---|
| | star | 5 |
| | star of David | 3 |
| | star jasmine | 1 |
| | Ninja star | 2 |
| | snowflake | 5 |
| | jack | 3 |
| | jelly fish | 1 |
| | star of Bethlehem | 2 |
| | starfish | 4 |

| Round 5: | | |
|---|---|---|
| | basket | 2 |
| | pail | 4 |
| | purse | 4 |
| | bag | 2 |
| | handbag | 5 |
| | hip hugger | 3 |
| | bucket | 1 |

| Round 6: | | |
|---|---|---|
| | strainer | 1 |
| | basket | 3 |
| | sieve | 4 |
| | sifter | 5 |
| | net | 4 |
| | deep fryer basket | 2 |
| | colander | 1 |

| Round 7: | | |
|---|---|---|
| | survey | 2 |
| | tripod | 3 |
| | level | 4 |
| | transit | 1 |
| | telescope | 5 |

| Round 8: | | |
|---|---|---|
| | pencil | 4 |
| | nail | 2 |
| | microphone | 5 |
| | spike | 3 |
| | eye dropper | 3 |
| | baster | 1 |

## Living in the Hearing World

1. Her flight was supposed to depart from Gate 10, but the airline changed the boarding gate at the last minute. Carlene was not informed of the change, even though she had notified the agent at the counter that she is Deaf. When she noticed that there were few people around, she checked with the agent again, but was reassured. Later on, she checked again and showed her ticket to make sure the agent understood her concern. It was then that the agent realized her flight was leaving from a different gate. Carlene raced to make the flight, but it had already left.

2. First, she asked around, but many people didn't know where it was. She finally found someone who said it might be near the car rental area. Sure enough, that's where it was.

3. The battery was dead.

4. She had to ask someone to make a voice call to the relay service, who would then make the TTY call to her boyfriend. It seemed that the message was relayed.

5. To her surprise, nearly 1,000 people attended the bowling tournament.

6. At first, she didn't recognize him, but when he smiled, she knew who he was. He is now bald, is still working and has two children.

## The Story Corner: "Uncoding the Ethics"

One afternoon a Deaf man noticed his neighbor digging a hole in his yard, placing a bag in the hole, and covering it with dirt. He thought the bag contained money but felt it was not well hidden, so early the next morning he got up and moved the bag to a safer location. Later that morning, the hearing neighbor got up to check on his money. In horror he saw the bag was gone, then noticed footprints leading to the house of his Deaf neighbor. He then knew who stole the money. He decided to call a Sign Language interpreter. When the interpreter arrived, she found out the missing bag contained $20,000. Then they both walked over to the neighbor's house, the man carrying his shotgun along. The interpreter related to the Deaf man why his neighbor was accusing him of taking the money. The Deaf man then explained he was doing him a favor by hiding it in a safe place. After the neighbor demanded to know where he hid the money, the Deaf man signed that he hid it under a rock by the tree. But the interpreter said that the Deaf man refused to say where he hid it. So, in the end, the interpreter was the only one left alive who knew where the money was.

(Certified Sign Language interpreters who are members of the Registry of Interpreters for the Deaf follow a Code of Ethics, part of which says that interpreters should transmit everything that is said or signed as accurately as possible—hence the title "Uncoding the Ethics.")

## CUMULATIVE REVIEW: UNITS 13–17

### Which Number Was That?

1. 12:50
2. 111
3. Nov. 2, 1992
4. June 7, 1938
5. 1520s
6. 10¢
7. 1:15
8. $3.00
9. 47 Freider
10. 200 Vella
11. 21 Londen
12. 36 Walden

### The Story Corner: "We Got Plenty of Them Back Home"

Russian: vodka
Cuban: cigars
Deaf man: hearing people

This joke was adapted to comment on the Deaf experience. In the original joke told among hearing people, an American threw a lawyer off the train, with the claim that we have plenty of them back home.

*End of Answer Key*

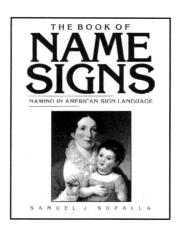

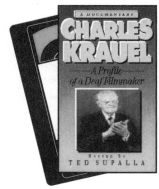

## Experience the Feelings and Emotions

In this inspiring collection of Deaf poetry, Ella Mae Lentz brings you eleven of her most memorable poems, beautifully presented in full color. This collection traces the development of Ella's style. It begins with her original works in written English which were later translated into ASL, and continues to her more recently composed works in ASL.

**The Treasure** *by Ella Mae Lentz*
One 60-minute Video ◆ voice-over

## "Baird's Art Makes Us Think, Analyze, Inspect, And Examine a Deaf Individual's Approach to Life."

This magnificent color book brings you thirty-five of Chuck Baird's most stunning paintings. They include some of his earlier works from private collections depicting mostly Deaf culture themes. Here you will meet Chuck Baird as a Deaf person and as an artist. With descriptive material about the artist and his work, every page shows the artist's interpretation of familiar, everyday surroundings.

**Chuck Baird: 35 PLATES** *Text by L. K. Elion*
64 pages ◆ 8½ x 10

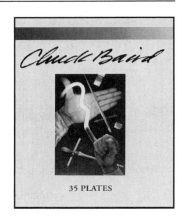

You are proud of your new expensive watch that has all the latest features. You can program it so that it will beep at specific times. Unfortunately, you never know when it beeps.

## More Hilarious Than Ever!

Published in the past as *Hazards of Deafness,* and *Silence is Golden, Sometimes,* the third and newest edition titled **DEAF CULTURE,** *Our Way* is now back by popular demand! Roy Holcomb and his sons, Sam and Tom, give an entertaining glimpse of life in the Deaf community that every reader will relate to. **DEAF CULTURE,** *Our Way* stands alone as an excellent collection of enjoyable anecdotes for both Deaf and hearing people alike. This all-time favorite now features contemporary hazards focusing even more on the humorous aspects of the Deaf experience. This hilarious compilation will instill in the reader a communion that no formal textbooks can ever accomplish!

**DEAF CULTURE,** *Our Way*
*by Roy, Sam, and Tom Holcomb*
128 pages ◆ 6" x 6"

## SPELLBOUND!
## Warm Up Your Hands... Exercise Your Eyes... Stretch Your Fingers!

Improve your fingerspelling through *Fingerspelling, Expressive & Receptive Fluency* by Joyce Linden Groode. In seven sections, the videotape along with a 24-page booklet demonstrates proper handshapes and techniques for both expressive and receptive skills. Included in the booklet is a self-test and fingerspelling practice activities. Using natural interactive process, Groode's lessons are voiced and closed-captioned for all audiences.

**Fingerspelling,** *Expressive & Receptive Fluency*
One 120-minute Video ◆ closed-captioned ◆ voice-over
includes a 24-page video guide booklet

FLO72

DAWNSIGNPRESS ◆ 6130 Nancy Ridge Drive, San Diego, California 92121-3223 ◆ ORDER TOLL FREE 1-800-549-5350 V/TTY

# WE HOPE YOU ENJOYED THIS BOOK...

DAWNSIGNPRESS is a specialty publisher for instructional sign language and educational Deaf Studies materials for both children and adults, deaf and hearing. Our portfolio of materials includes exciting books and videotapes on sign language, children's stories, Deaf culture, as well as school curriculum materials.

*If you would like to know more about DAWNSIGNPRESS products, please complete the following information and send it to us.*

Name: _____

Address: _____

City/State/Zip: _____

Phone: ( _____ ) _____

*How did you like this workbook?*

_____

_____

_____

_____

*Please send my friend a catalog.*

Name: _____

Address: _____

City/State/Zip: _____

# DAWNSIGNPRESS

6130 Nancy Ridge Drive, San Diego, California 92121-3223

(619) 626-0600 V/TTY   (619) 625-2336 FAX

ORDER TOLL FREE 1-800-549-5350 V/TTY

FL072

# ORDER FORM

## BILL TO:

NAME _____

ADDRESS ❑ Home ❑ Work _____

CITY/STATE/ZIP _____

PHONE ❑ Voice ❑ TTY _____

## SHIP TO: *(if different)*

NAME _____

PROGRAM/DEPT. _____

ADDRESS ❑ Home ❑ Work *(no P.O. boxes please)*

CITY/STATE/ZIP _____

PHONE ❑ Voice ❑ TTY _____

| Item # | DESCRIPTION | PRICE | QTY | TOTAL |
|---|---|---|---|---|
| | Catalog | | 1 | Free |
| 2228 | *The Book of Name Signs* | $12.95 | | |
| 3650 | *A Journey into the Deaf-World* (hardback) | $39.95 | | |
| 3652 | *A Journey into the Deaf-World* (paperback) | $24.95 | | |
| 9601V | *ASL Poetry, Selected Works of Clayton Valli* | $29.95 | | |
| 9111V | *Charles Krauel, A Profile of a Deaf Filmmaker* | $29.95 | | |
| 9664V | *The Treasure* | $39.95 | | |
| 2341 | *Chuck Baird, 35 Plates* | $22.00 | | |
| 2226 | *Deaf Culture, Our Way* | $ 8.95 | | |
| 2202 | *Fingerspelling, Expressive & Receptive Fluency* | $39.95 | | |

### METHOD OF PAYMENT

❑ Check or Money Order enclosed # _____

(Make check payable to DawnSignPress; all payments must be in US dollars.)

❑ Charge: ❑ VISA ❑ MasterCard Exp. Date: _____

| | | | | | | | | | | | | | | | |
|--|--|--|--|--|--|--|--|--|--|--|--|--|--|--|--|

Cardholder Name: _____

Signature: _____
*Signature required for credit cards.*

Subtotal _____

(for CA residents only) 7.25% sales tax _____

(for Canadian residents only) 7% GST _____

Shipping & Handling ____ **FREE**

**Total Enclosed** _____

**To order, duplicate this page and fax or mail to:**

DawnSignPress
6130 Nancy Ridge Drive, San Diego, California 92121-3223
(619) 626-0600 V/TTY  (619) 625-2336 FAX
ORDER TOLL FREE 1-800-549-5350 V/TTY

*Purchase policy:  All orders from individuals must be pre-paid in U.S. dollars. All orders from schools, libraries and bookstores must be accompanied by payment, a purchase order, or other signed authorization. Terms NET 30 days. Prices subject to change without notice. Please allow 1-2 weeks for processing and shipment of your order (longer for international orders). All shipments via UPS with the exception of orders under $200 to Hawaii, Alaska, and Canada. No P.O. boxes, please.*

FL072

# notes

# notes

# notes

# notes

# notes

# notes